D1266405

Wargaming:
19th Century Europe
1815–1878

Wargaming:
19th Century Europe
1815–1878

NEIL THOMAS

Pen & Sword
MILITARY

First published in Great Britain in 2012 by
PEN & SWORD MILITARY
An imprint of
Pen & Sword Books Ltd
47 Church Street
Barnsley
South Yorkshire
S70 2AS

ISBN 978-1-84884-629-6

A CIP catalogue record for this book is
available from the British Library

Typeset by Concept, Huddersfield, West Yorkshire.
Printed and bound in England by CPI Group (UK) Ltd, Croydon, CR0 4YY.

Pen & Sword Books Ltd incorporates the Imprints of Pen & Sword Aviation,
Pen & Sword Maritime, Pen & Sword Military, Wharncliffe Local History,
Pen & Sword Select, Pen & Sword Military Classics, Leo Cooper,
Remember When, Seaforth Publishing and Frontline Publishing

For a complete list of Pen & Sword titles please contact
PEN & SWORD BOOKS LIMITED
47 Church Street, Barnsley, South Yorkshire, S70 2AS, England
E-mail: enquiries@pen-and-sword.co.uk
Website: www.pen-and-sword.co.uk

Contents

Acknowledgements vi
List of Plates vii
List of Maps x
Key to Symbols xi
Introduction xii

 1. Nineteenth-Century Warfare 1
 2. Nineteenth-Century Wargaming 23
 3. Nineteenth-Century Wargames Rules 42
 4. Wargames Scenarios 50
 5. Wargames Army Lists 61
 6. Wargaming Historical Battles 89
 7. The Battle of Alegria (17 October 1834) 92
 8. The Battle of Oriamendi (16 March 1837) 97
 9. The Battle of the Alma (20 September 1854) 104
10. The Battle of Montebello (20 May 1859) 113
11. The Battle of Oeversee (6 February 1864) 122
12. The Battle of Rackebull (17 March 1864) 130
13. The Battle of Nachod (27 June 1866) 137
14. The Battle of Kissingen (10 July 1866) 147
15. The Battle of Mars-La-Tour (16 August 1870) 155
16. The Battle of Sedan (1 September 1870) 166

Appendix 1: Bibliography 174
Appendix 2: Figure Sizes, Scales and Prices 185
Appendix 3: Useful Addresses 188
Index 192

Acknowledgements

I would like to thank my father, Kaye Thomas, for typing the manuscript for this book. Also to everyone at Pen & Sword Books, especially Philip Sidnell, whose enthusiasm for, and commitment to, this project have proved invaluable.

This book has benefitted greatly from the magnificent colour photographs that grace the plate section. I would therefore like to thank all who have supplied the images, namely Peter Berry of Baccus 6mm Ltd; master figure painter Kevin Dallimore; Peter Johnstone of Spencer Smith Miniatures; editor Andrew Hubback and photographer Richard Ellis of *Miniature Wargames* magazine; Duncan Rogers of Helion & Company (whose figures are now owned and sold by Nick Eyre of North Star Military Figures Ltd); and Ralph Weaver of The Continental Wars Society.

Finally, any writers on wargaming this epoch must record their debt to the just mentioned Continental Wars Society, and especially to John Pocock and Ralph Weaver, whose pioneering work have done so much to promote the fascinating period covered by this book.

List of Plates

1. The Polish Insurrection (1831). Polish rebels await their Russian foes from behind a barricade.

2. 'Steady Boys!' The mounted Polish general encourages his men to stand firm.

3. The First Carlist War (1833–1837). The Carlist forces attack a village held by their Cristino enemies.

4. 'To the bayonet!' The Cristino infantry charges its foe.

5. The Battle of Miloslaw (1848). The Poles fight for their freedom again, this time against a Prussian force.

6. The Polish patriots assault the Prussian lines.

7. Radetzky's march. The Austrian army launches a concerted assault upon the Italians at the Battle of Novara (1849).

8. The somewhat demoralised Italians await the Austrian onslaught at Novara.

9. The Charge of the Light Brigade. The remnant of the British 17th Lancers approaches the Russian guns at the Battle of Balaclava (1854).

10. The Crimean War (1854–1856). French forces defend a river against a Russian assault.

11. The crisis point of the battle is reached, with the French preparing to repel the Russian attack.

12. Wargame conventions allow for the display of massive wargames. This game uses 15mm figures to depict the French and Austrian armies clashing at the Battle of Solferino (1859). It was presented by the Newbury and Reading Wargames Society.

13. Another view of the Solferino wargame.

14. This group of Prussian infantry wears the feldmutz field cap, rather than the more famous pickelhaube helmet.

15. A unit of Prussian uhlans on patrol.

16. The wrong way to do it. This Austrian storm column from the Seven Weeks War is about to be destroyed by Prussian fire-power.

17. The right way to try it. These Austrian infantrymen have formed a firing line.

18. The Austrian cavalry was the pride of the 1866 army. This is a unit of hussars.

19. The Krupp rifled artillery proved decisive during the Franco-Prussian War (1870–1871). This Bavarian example was painted by Kevin Dallimore.

20. This Franco-Prussian clash shows the Prussian cavalry about to dispose of its French counterparts.

21. The Prussian infantry assaults the French village.

22. 6mm figures allow for wargames to be fought on very small tables. This French army is designed to be used with my rules.

23. A Prussian 6mm army configured for my rules.

24. The Battle of Gravelotte–St Privat (1870). The right wing of the Prussian Guard Corps is about to be shattered when attacking St Privat.

25. The Prussian Guard Corps' central component launches a diversionary attack.

26. The decisive blow. The success of the left wing of the Prussian Guards led to the capture of Roncourt – and the subsequent outflanking of the French line.

27. The French defenders of Roncourt await their fate.

28. The Battle of Loigny–Poupry (1870). The French advance on Loigny.

29. The French clash with Bavarian troops outside Loigny. Note how flags can aid unit recognition with diminutive miniatures.

30. The French centre at Loigny–Poupry encounters the Prussian advance guard outside the village of Lumeau.

31. The Prussian main body deploys behind Lumeau, ready to reinforce the advance guard.

32. A Prussian division deploys from marching column into a firing line.

33. This French infantry unit has every intention of relying on the firepower of its Chassepot rifles.

List of Maps

1. A Suggested Battlefield: Scenarios 1–4   52
2. A Suggested Battlefield: Scenario 5   58
3. The Battle of Alegria   94
4. The Battle of Oriamendi 101
5. The Battle of the Alma 110
6. The Battle of Montebello 119
7. The Battle of Oeversee 126
8. The Battle of Rackebull 133
9. The Battle of Nachod 143
10. The Battle of Kissingen 150
11. The Battle of Mars-La-Tour 162
12. The Battle of Sedan 171

Key to Symbols

The maps in this book make use of the following symbols:

⊠ ◪ = Infantry

⊠ ◪ = Skirmishers

◸ ◪ = Cavalry

⊥ = Artillery

⬭ = Hill

⬬ = Wood

▦ = Town

⊓ = Redoubt

〜 = Stream or River

⬮ = Lake

═ = Road

▰▰▰ = Railway

⏝ = Bridge

⋯ = Ford

(Obj) = Objective

Ⓐ = Entry Point

Introduction

This book follows on from my earlier work on *Napoleonic Wargaming*; the period which it covers should not in any way be seen as an afterthought. For the nineteenth century was even more significant than the Napoleonic age: the French Emperor's epoch may have been spectacular, but Napoleon's political project ended in complete failure. The nineteenth century was very different: its politics saw the shaping of modern Europe with the creation of the new nation states of Italy and Germany; its industrial revolution led in turn to a military revolution, with the developments of railways and sophisticated breechloading weaponry helping foster the growth of large, technologically advanced armies. All these developments happened between 1815 and 1878; this is the first wargames book entirely devoted to exploring this decisive epoch.

The work begins with a chapter exploring all the significant military and political developments of the period. I then provide a chapter explaining the parameters governing my rules, and the principles behind them. This should be a vital part of any set of wargames rules, since it allows all wargamers to understand what motivated the designer. The rules themselves come next; they are intentionally simple, yet can be relied upon to deliver historically viable outcomes – an approach which is intended to maximise enjoyment whilst enhancing understanding.

The book then proceeds along a different path to my previous offerings, by providing five different types of scenario for the wargamer to enjoy. The first four of these – pitched battle, meeting engagement, rearguard action, and flank attack – provide noteworthy generic types of encounter, all of which are designed to deliver challenges for the wargamer. They are also intended to be physically manageable, taking place as they do on areas of 120cm (4') × 90cm (3'); most living room tables are at least of this size. The fifth scenario is a minigame; this is a pitched battle fought over an area of 60cm (2') × 60cm (2'): it is intended for wargamers with extremely restricted playing areas, or very small armies. I have provided twenty-eight army lists for the period, covering all the most significant forces: players should easily be able to find a favourite army to play any scenario.

I have also included details of nine historical battles to be fought as wargames, with dedicated army lists and special rules for each encounter. These are again intended to be fought over small areas; seven are designed for tables of 120cm × 90cm, and two for areas of just 60cm × 60cm. These allow the wargamer to change the course of history within the four walls of his or her own home – a seductive prospect for all players to savour.

As with my previous books, I have included Appendices containing supporting material. I begin with a Bibliography, which adds brief comments to each listed book, thereby explaining the content of each work and giving potential readers an idea of its likely utility. The sections on figure sizes (with a rough price guide) and useful addresses will be of use to all wargamers, but are especially directed at beginners – who may not be aware which products are available, and which may be most suitable.

Wargames set in nineteenth-century Europe allow players to decide the destiny of an entire continent. They can fight to realise the dreams of nationhood and liberty; or they may prefer defending order and tradition from the horrors of demagogic disorder and the mass hysteria of nationalism. The stakes could not be higher – are you ready for the challenge?

Chapter 1

Nineteenth-Century Warfare

KEY EVENTS

1815	Congress of Vienna. Nationalism and liberalism are repudiated as the old monarchical order is restored.
1820–1821	Neapolitan revolt. Crushed by Austrian army at the Battle of Rieti.
1820–1823	Rebellion in Spain. Defeated by French at the Battle of Trocadero.
1821–1829	Greek revolt. Independence from Ottoman rule secured following English, French and Russian military support for the insurgents.
1826–1834	Portuguese Civil War. Constitutionalists defeat absolutists thanks to English assistance.
1830	French Revolution. Bourbon dynasty replaced by Orleanists.
1830–1831	Polish insurrection. Suppressed by Russian army after dogged resistance.
1830–1833	War of Belgian Independence. Dutch rule overthrown following French intervention on Belgian side.
1833–1837	First Carlist War. Spanish government (assisted by the French Foreign Legion and a British Legion) defeats a rebellion led by the late king's brother, Don Carlos.
1848	French Revolution. Orleanist dynasty overthrown and replaced by Second Republic. Louis-Napoleon Bonaparte elected President.
1848–1849	German revolution suppressed by Prussians.
1848–1849	Austrian, Czech and Hungarian revolutions smashed by Hapsburg Empire.
1848–1849	Piedmontese bid to lead Italian revolt crushed by Hapsburgs at the Battles of Custoza and Novara.

1848–1850   First Schleswig War. Denmark defeats the attempt of Schleswig-Holstein to secure independence, despite the latter being assisted by the Prussian army.

1849   Roman Republic set up by Italian revolutionaries. Guiseppe Garibaldi plays a leading role in its defence, all to no avail as Papal authority is restored by French troops.

1850   Coup d'état in France. Louis-Napoleon Bonaparte institutes Second Empire, assuming the title of Napoleon III.

1854–1856   Crimean War. Britain, France and Piedmont invade the Crimea in a successful attempt to thwart Russian designs upon the Ottoman Empire.

1859   Franco-Austrian War. French expel Hapsburgs from Italy (except Venetia) following the Battle of Solferino.

1860   Garibaldi and a tiny force of 1,000 men expel the Neapolitan régime from Sicily.

1860–1861   Kingdom of Italy created after Garibaldi takes Naples and Piedmont seizes the Papal States (apart from Rome).

1864   Second Schleswig War. Prussia and Austria expel Danes from Schleswig-Holstein.

1866   Seven Weeks War (Italian campaign). Austrians defeat the Italians at the Battle of Custoza. However, the Hapsburgs are still forced to evacuate Venetia following events elsewhere (see next entry).

1866   Seven Weeks War (German campaign). Prussia defeats Austria at the Battle of Königgrätz, and secures predominance in Germany.

1870   Franco-Prussian War (Imperial phase). Prussia defeats France. Napoleon III deposed following his surrender at the Battle of Sedan. French Third Republic instituted.

1870   Italy united following the defeat of the Papal army in Rome.

1870–1871   Franco-Prussian War (Republican phase). The Prussians defeat a succession of French Republican attempts to raise the siege of Paris.

2

1871   German Empire created under leadership of Prussian monarchy. The formerly French provinces of Alsace and Lorraine are added to the new Imperial territories.

1872–1876   Second Carlist War. A second Don Carlos (grandson of the first) fails to reimpose an absolute monarchy in Spain.

1877–1878   Russo-Turkish War. Russia defeats the Ottoman Empire, creating Bulgaria as a result.

1878   Congress of Berlin. Germany and the Hapsburg Empire force Russia to agree a reduction in the size of Bulgaria. The Balkans remains a potential flashpoint in European diplomacy.

TURNING THE CLOCK BACK

Radicalism was a dirty word in 1815. The French Revolutionary principles of liberty, equality and international brotherhood were supposed to portend an epoch of reason, enlightenment and peace: they produced instead an era of dictatorship, hysteria and bloodshed. It is scarcely surprising that Europe heaved a collective sigh of relief when Napoleon I was finally defeated at Waterloo; or that the principles he claimed to espouse found themselves utterly discredited.

In accordance with these sentiments, the peace settlement agreed at Vienna in 1815 took on a distinctly reactionary hue. Its leading author, the Austrian Chancellor (Prime Minister) Prince Klemens von Metternich, aimed to recreate the old European order of the eighteenth century. His guiding principle lay in maintaining the balance of power. This meant a restoration of the power and privileges of the old European monarchies, which explained why the Bourbons returned to govern France; it also demanded that no single power was in a position to dominate its neighbours. Accordingly, Europe was carved up in the interests of international order, and was moreover done so successfully: there was no conflict between the major European powers until the Crimean War.

Power politics of this kind necessarily meant a repudiation of such revolutionary principles as liberalism and nationalism. Absolute monarchies such as Russia, Prussia, the (Austrian) Hapsburg Empire and the restored French Bourbon régime inevitably had

3

little time for any liberal challenge to despotic rule; even the dangerously radical (to European eyes) British constitutional monarchy only allowed a tiny minority of highly influential people to vote in parliamentary elections. As for nationalism, Metternich saw this as an even greater threat to order. This was because national sentiment bore little relation to the boundaries agreed at Vienna: for example, the Hapsburg Empire was a multinational entity that would be torn apart if its constituent peoples enjoyed autonomy; and the assorted small principalities that encompassed areas inhabited by Germans and Italians would lose their reason to exist if nationalistic sentiments were ever allowed to hold sway. Moreover, the creation of two large national entities in the place of several smaller ones would inevitably undermine the balance of power so delicately contrived at the Congress of Vienna.

It was particularly fitting that an Austrian politician played such a leading role in determining the new order. For the Hapsburg Empire played a central role in every sense: geographically, it occupied the middle of Europe; and in political terms, it defined the principles of the Congress, being a governmental construct based upon dynastic tradition and historical accident, rather than upon ideological concepts like nationalism and liberalism. The Vienna settlement would stand or fall according to the fortunes of the Hapsburg Empire.

In essence, the Congress of Vienna stood for the eighteenth-century values of enlightened despotism. Metternich himself was not wholly opposed to all political reform (provided that any changes strengthened the existing order), and he disliked the revival of Catholic clerical conservatism after 1815 almost as much as he abhorred democratic sentiments. Accordingly, some changes to the Vienna system were tolerated at the margins. Thus it was that the Greek revolt against Ottoman Turkish rule was supported, since the new state became a part of the European rather than the Asiatic orbit; a constitutional monarchy was allowed to develop in France; and the sundering of Belgium from Dutch rule was tolerated on condition that the new state remained politically neutral. The key factor behind the Vienna settlement was always going to be international stability: crushing nationalistic and radical liberal agitation was its focus.

SMALL IS BEAUTIFUL

The political imperatives outlined above had a major effect upon military developments, in particular the size of military establishments. Large armies were regarded as an especially dangerous Napoleonic innovation, for example. These required mass mobilisations, which potentially entailed recruiting middle class officers of a liberal persuasion whose loyalty to the old order was far from assured. Large forces were also in a position to invade potentially weaker neighbours, which would serve to undermine Metternich's carefully wrought balance of power.

These rather apocalyptic prospects were averted by the revival of small, professional armies on the eighteenth-century pattern. These could be officered by the nobility, whose loyalty to their king was assured; as a result, the army could be relied upon to suppress any revolutionary uprising with uncompromising brutality. Moreover, small armies were not in a position to launch large scale invasions of major powers; expeditions to restore or support an embattled neighbouring monarchy represented the principal variety of foreign military adventure.

The practical results of all this took the form of a bastardised Napoleonic approach; the erstwhile Emperor's strategic and tactical maxims were adopted, but the mass armies of the Napoleonic Wars were eschewed. This synthesis of Enlightenment and Napoleonic principles was to find its theorist in Antoine Henri Jomini, a Swiss officer who spent much of the Napoleonic Wars serving in the French army, only to change sides and join the Russians in 1813. His *Summary of the Art of War* (1830) proved highly influential, advocating as it did the desirability of limited rather than total warfare:

> Without being a utopian philanthropist or a professional soldier, a person may desire that wars of extermination may be banished from the code of nations ... I acknowledge that my prejudices are in favour of the good old times when the French and English Guards courteously invited each other to fire first – as at Fontenoy (1745) – preferring them to the frightful epoch when priests, women and children throughout Spain plotted the murder of isolated soldiers (1808–1814).
>
> Antoine Henri Jomini (1830) 'Summary of the Art of War' in
> *Roots of Strategy Book 2*, Stackpole Books, 1987, p. 446.

It was fitting that Jomini's preference for moderation found its expression in his enthusiasm for the sort of intricate strategic manoeuvre that was such a feature of eighteenth-century warfare. Accordingly, Jomini placed great stress upon occupying strategic points, thereby putting the enemy at a severe disadvantage. His book goes into great detail about exactly how this desirable end can be achieved, but it does express the overall aim in a single maxim:

> To throw by strategic movements the mass of the army, successively, upon the decisive points of a theatre of war, and also upon the communications of an enemy as much as possible without compromising one's own.
>
> Antoine Henri Jomini (1830) 'Summary of the Art of War' in
> *Roots of Strategy Book 2*, Stackpole Books, 1987, p. 461.

Jomini's strategical preferences may have been for manoeuvre on the eighteenth-century pattern; his tactical programme did by contrast owe everything to Napoleon, especially with respect to infantry. For the eighteenth century saw its foot soldiers deployed in long lines with a depth of two or three ranks (usually the latter). These could deliver a great volume of fire, since every man could shoot his musket, but were doomed to marching very slowly, given the problems of maintaining alignment when minor obstacles constantly had to be traversed by part of the formation. The Napoleonic Wars saw a very different technique come to the fore. All armies used line formation in defence, where maximum firepower was more important than rapid movement; but attacking infantry often adopted a columnar approach. Here, the foot soldiers were deployed in deeper (anything from six to twenty-four ranks) but narrower formations. These could move far more rapidly than lines, since they could march around obstacles rather than have to force their way through them.

The use of infantry columns made rapid assaults more feasible. Their attack would be assisted by an artillery bombardment intended to weaken the defenders; and their approach march preceded by light infantry skirmishers in open order, which would indulge in sniping at the enemy. This fire would have little material effect, thanks to the weaknesses of the notoriously inaccurate musket, which only started to inflict significant damage at a range of about 50 yards. However, the combination of artillery and skirmishers could weaken morale, so that the approach of a homicidally inclined enemy column would cause the defenders to flee. If however they stood their ground, the attackers would lose their ardour and either run away themselves, or deploy into line formation to indulge in a musketry duel with the defenders. The ultimate victor would be the army with the greatest morale – which could of course be greatly assisted by such factors as numerical superiority, or deployment behind cover.

Cavalry played a vital support role both in attack and defence. It would deploy in successive lines (three waves was typical) with sufficient intervals between each to prevent any catastrophic collisions. The chief value of the horse lay in its mobility: attacking units could charge a wavering enemy, forcing it to run away; they could launch a mass assault upon a retreating army, turning a defeat into a rout. Cavalry also had a vital role in defence: it could move rapidly to a point where the enemy threatened to break through, and launch a charge in order to win time for other reinforcements to retrieve the situation; or it could counter attack enemy troops whose assault had been halted by friendly musketry, thereby turning the tables on the foe. It must however be stressed that cavalry was chiefly a supporting weapon: horses simply could not be forced to charge an unbroken enemy. A steady body of infantry in close order line or column formation combined as it was with the effect of musketry, would quell any cavalry charge upon its frontal face. Steady foot soldiers were only really vulnerable to charges upon their flanks – an unfortunate possibility which could always be thwarted by the infantry forming a square, a formation which by definition could never be outflanked. Nor would cavalry charge its enemy counterparts; provided that both sides were in good order, they would shy away from each other before contact.

Cavalry was therefore a limited weapon. It could nevertheless have a devastating effect when unleashed upon a wavering foe: for the latter would flee before contact, resulting in terrible slaughter as the cavalry charged home. The role of horsemen on the battlefield was summed up by Jomini:

> Whatever may be its importance in the ensemble of the operations of war, cavalry can never defend a position without the support of infantry. Its chief duty is to open the way for gaining

a victory, or to render it complete by carrying off prisoners and trophies, pursuing the enemy, rapidly succouring a threatened point, overthrowing disordered infantry, covering retreats of infantry and artillery. An army deficient in cavalry rarely obtains a great victory, and finds its retreats extremely difficult.

Antoine Henri Jomini (1830) 'Summary of the Art of War' in
Roots of Strategy, Book 2, Stackpole Books, 1987, p. 547.

Success on the post-Napoleonic battlefield required the imaginative use of infantry, cavalry, and artillery in combination. All this was possible with the small professional armies that were effectively mandated by the Congress of Vienna. However, political change and technical innovation were soon to change the military scene in a startling manner.

1848: THE FAILURE OF LIBERALISM

Metternichian conservation may have been popular with the aristocratic ruling élites; it was loathed both by middle class professionals, and the industrialists who were beginning to make their mark upon Europe. This grouping stood for liberal principles, and laid great stress upon fundamental rights rather than entrenched privileges. They stood for such notions as equality before the law; freedom of speech; freedom of worship; freedom of assembly; freedom of the press; and freedom from arbitrary arrest or imprisonment. More broadly, liberals demanded a constitution incorporating a form of parliamentary government.

These demands, expressed as they often were with somewhat intoxicating rhetoric, may have proved spectacularly unwelcome to the old order – but were in fact quite moderate in scope. In essence, the rising middle classes wanted some power for themselves: the proposed parliaments were only to be elected by a minority of the populace, and the fundamental rights the liberals saw as inalienable contained absolutely no mention of the redistribution of wealth. Nineteenth-century liberals were appalled by the very notion of any outside interference with the wheels of commerce; any measures implemented to control economic exploitation were invariably introduced by those conservatives who saw it as their duty to help the poor.

The limitations of liberalism help to explain why it was usually the preserve of a vocal minority. However, economic distress could occasionally broaden its appeal. Thus it was that 1848 saw a mass revolutionary upsurge across Europe, following a food shortage after a run of bad harvests, and an industrial crisis sparked by overproduction (this occurs when firms produce a large quantity of goods during an economic boom, only for the supply to eventually exceed demand, leading to a slump). The outbreak of revolutionary activity met with initial successes; the French monarchy was replaced by a Republic; Metternich was forced into exile; and in the Italian territories, the Kingdom of Piedmont led an attempt to expel the Hapsburgs.

The revolutionaries' good fortune did not last. For, as has already been observed, liberalism was the creed of a minority: it simply lacked the sustained mass support necessary to make it endure. As a result, the professional armies created by the Vienna settlement were able to crush the revolutionary mobs with some ease; and in Italy, the Hapsburg army proved itself infinitely superior to that of Piedmont.

The events of 1848 had shown that liberalism was something of a paper tiger, and not only because it lacked any popular basis. A greater problem was its failure to display any international solidarity: liberals were also nationalists, and they showed a distinct tendency to support the old order when it suppressed revolutions elsewhere. The phenomenon was most notably observed when German revolutionaries cheered on the Hapsburg armies, when they crushed the Slav rebels in Bohemia. This tendency for nationalism to convert liberals into conservatives was to have significant political ramifications during the second half of the nineteenth century. Of more immediate concern to the old order was the gradual rise of industry, which presented a serious political threat.

THE INDUSTRIAL CHALLENGE
The nineteenth century saw the gradual development of a new economic order. Industrialisation may only have been fully entrenched in Britain and Belgium by 1848, but it was beginning to gain a toehold in France and some parts of Germany (chiefly those which fell into the Prussian political orbit). By the end of the century, Germany was fully industrialised; France and Italy had significant areas dominated by factories; and even Russia, always the most backward part of Europe, was starting to develop heavy industry.

The spread of industry inevitably meant the growth of an urban working class, which presented a whole new political problem. For economic growth was often achieved at the expense of poor working conditions, which in turn led to the rise of socialism. Workers not unnaturally saw that they had few friends amongst their employers, and therefore started to embrace radical political causes.

The most uncompromising of these new theories was communism. In many ways, the publication of Karl Marx and Friedrich Engels' *The Communist Manifesto* was the most significant event of 1848, giving expression as it did to the creed which was to prove so enormously influential over the following 150 years. The tone of the entire document is utterly uncompromising: Marx and Engels maintained that social classes had always been irreconcilably opposed, a condition that was moreover even clearer in the era of industrial capitalism:

> The history of all hitherto existing society is the history of class struggles ... Our epoch, the epoch of the bourgeoisie, possesses, however, this distinctive feature: it has simplified the class antagonisms. Society as a whole is more and more splitting up into two great hostile camps, into two great classes directly facing each other: Bourgeoisie and Proletariat.
>
> Marx, Karl and Engels, Friedrich (1848) 'The Communist Manifesto' in Marx and Engels, *Selected Works*, Lawrence and Wishart, 1968, pp. 35–6.

Marx and Engels had noted how industrialisation had given birth to exceptionally harsh working conditions in the new factories. They maintained that this stemmed from the necessity of maximising profit in any capitalist system, and that the old values of Christian charity and responsibility to help the poor were therefore dead:

> The bourgeoisie, wherever it has got the upper hand, has put an end to all feudal, patriarchal, idyllic relations. It has pitilessly torn asunder the motley feudal ties that bound man to his 'natural superiors', and has left remaining no other nexus between man and man than naked self-interest, than callous 'cash payment' ... In one word, for exploitation, veiled by religious and political illusions, it has substituted naked, shameless, direct, brutal exploitation.
>
> Marx, Karl and Engels, Friedrich (1848) 'The Communist Manifesto' in Marx and Engels, *Selected Works*, Lawrence and Wishart, 1968, p. 38.

The combative tone of this rhetoric is striking: Marx and Engels were certainly no pacifists – indeed, Engels was himself an astute and respected military commentator. Communism proved to be a threat to all governments; and when it gained power in Russia and elsewhere during the twentieth century, revealed itself to be utterly ruthless and appallingly brutal towards any perceived political opponent. During the nineteenth century however, Communism appeared to be the voice of the oppressed – and there was certainly much to complain about, for the conduct of many factory owners was inexcusable. Accordingly, it was imperative for the old monarchies to win the allegiance of the newly created working class.

NATIONALISM: THE DOUBLE-EDGED SWORD

The political challenge presented by industrialisation led in due course to a re-evaluation of nationalism on the part of the European monarchies. It will be recalled that the Vienna settlement was predicated on hostility to nationalist views: these were seen as the evil twin of liberalism, producing a combination that would undermine the Hapsburg Empire, thereby threatening European political stability.

This traditional view saw itself challenged as a result of the 1848 revolutions. Authoritarian régimes such as the Prussian monarchy observed that their military suppression of the Slav revolutionaries in Bohemia met with the enthusiastic support of German liberals. Accordingly, it was becoming clear that international liberal solidarity was decidedly weak, whereas nationalistic sentiments were much stronger – even to the extent of supporting reactionary monarchies whose armies were seen to act in the national interest.

The second half of the nineteenth century saw the enactment of this analysis, with the overthrow of the Vienna settlement. Its continued survival was seen to be in the interests of the Hapsburgs alone: The French Second Empire, and the Kings of Prussia and Piedmont had more to gain from reinventing themselves as defenders of their respective nations. All managed to achieve some successes (although Napoleon III miscalculated spectacularly when choosing to go to war with Prussia in 1870, and lost power as a result). Indeed, the Prussian and Piedmontese monarchies were to become the rulers of Germany and Italy respectively. This startling ability to neutralise liberal and egalitarian sentiment was noted by the French military thinker Ardant du Picq, who observed of the Prussians:

> The King of Prussia and the Prussian nobility, threatened by democracy, have had to change the passion for equality in their people into a passion for domination over foreign nations. This is easily done, when domination is crowned with success, for man, who is merely the friend of equality is the lover of domination.
>
> Ardant du Picq (1880) 'Battle Studies' in *Roots of Strategy, Book 2*,
> Stackpole Books, 1987, p. 243.

Some European monarchies were therefore able to reinvigorate themselves when their kings posed as fathers of the nation. Imaginative ministers such as Otto von Bismarck of Prussia helped cement this by introducing limited welfare legislation: for conservatives, unlike liberals, never had any ideological problem about interfering with individual rights for the greater good of society.

THE POLITICISATION OF WARFARE

The conservative embrace of nationalism was to have significant implications for warfare. For conflict was now going to be between peoples rather than states: war was now seen almost as an existential struggle, with national honour at stake. Accordingly, the nature of warfare changed from the limited approach postulated by the Congress of Vienna; mobilisation of nations implied a much larger scale of conflict than a dynastic argument over a minor border province.

These developments had significant theoretical implications. What could be described as the Jominian preference for limited warfare was now obsolete, and was replaced by the doctrines of his great contemporary, the Prussian Carl von Clausewitz. The latter would not have been surprised when the new political order had military ramifications, for his great work *On War* had always stressed that warfare was never separate from politics, but was actually subordinate to it:

> It is, of course, well known that the only source of war is politics – the intercourse of governments and peoples; but it is apt to be assumed that war suspends that intercourse and replaces it by a

wholly different condition, ruled by no law but its own. We maintain, on the contrary, that war is simply a continuation of political intercourse, with the addition of other means ... War cannot be divorced from political life; and whenever this occurs in our thinking about war, the many links that connect the two elements are destroyed and we are left with something pointless and devoid of sense.

> Carl von Clausewitz (1832) *On War*, translated by
> Michael Howard and Peter Paret, Princeton, 1976, p. 605.

Clausewitz was fully conscious that the Napoleonic Wars had wrought both political and military changes of the greatest magnitude. He was especially aware that the notion of limited warfare that Jomini hoped to resurrect was a fallacy:

> War is thus an act of force to compel our enemy to do our will ... Kind-hearted people might of course think there was some ingenious way to disarm or defeat an enemy without too much bloodshed, and might imagine this is the true goal of the art of war. Pleasant as it sounds, it is a fallacy that must be exposed: war is such a dangerous business that the mistakes which come from kindness are the very worst ... It would be futile – even wrong – to try to shut one's eyes to what war really is from sheer distress at its brutality.

> Carl von Clausewitz (1932) *On War*, translated by
> Michael Howard and Peter Paret, Princeton, 1976, pp. 75–76.

This uncompromising view of warfare was much in keeping with the nationalistic imperatives. These entailed large scale struggles between peoples, who embodied the nation, which would necessarily become exceptionally bloody. Accordingly, the Jominian emphasis on manoeuvre and the occupation of strategic points, become a relic of a bygone age. Clausewitz maintained instead that the sole aim of warfare was to destroy the enemy army: everything else was secondary:

> Our discussion has shown that while in war many different roads can lead to the goal, to the attainment of the political object, fighting is the only possible means. Everything is governed by a supreme law, the decision by force of arms ... To

sum up: of all the possible aims in war the destruction of the enemy's armed forces always appears as the highest.

Carl von Clausewitz (1932) On War, translated by
Michael Howard and Peter Paret, Princeton, 1976, p. 99.

Clausewitzian doctrine therefore entailed a war of annihilation in an unrestrained attempt to destroy the enemy army. Its combination with the nationalistic concept of a truly popular war implied the development of large armies in turn. Fortunately for the proponents of such views, the very industrial civilisation that proved such a potential threat to the old political order, also allowed for the creation of a substantial military establishment.

INDUSTRIAL OPPORTUNITIES
It will be recalled that the Vienna settlement led to the repudiation of the large armies that were such a feature of the Napoleonic Wars. Although this was a political decision, there were some very good logistical arguments against mass mobilisation. In essence, the supply arrangements of the early nineteenth century could not cope with providing for large armies; long marches would result in serious attrition; and the inability of mounted couriers to transmit orders quickly over long distances meant that forces had to be concentrated in relatively small areas – which tended to increase the losses that inevitably accrued from infectious diseases.

The results of this rather gloomy litany were seen in their starkest form during Napoleon's invasion of Russia, a campaign which saw the Grande Armée being reduced from 600,000 to just 50,000. It was apparent that the Napoleonic expedient of supplementing the supply network by living off the land was of distinctly limited utility, especially if the enemy adopted a 'scorched earth' policy of burning crops before Napoleon's men could get their hands on them.

This situation had changed markedly by the time that authoritarian nationalism made its mark from 1848 onwards. Two innovations made mass mobilisation possible. The first of these was the railway. This ended the need for a long approach march to the theatre of operations, so that armies could now concentrate for battle within two weeks rather than two months. Moreover, recently recruited conscripts or reservists would no longer be decimated thanks to the punishing demands of route marches. The more advanced military commanders were fully aware of the significance and potential of railways in warfare for, as the Prussian Field Marshal von Moltke observed:

> Every new development of railways is a military advantage; and for the national defence a few million on the completion of our railways is far more profitably employed than on our new fortresses.
>
> Helmuth von Moltke, quoted in Howard, Michael,
> *The Franco-Prussian War*, Routledge, 2002 (originally 1961), p. 2.

The railway network made it possible to allow for the deployment of large armies without suffering substantial losses from attrition. However, it was imperative that orders be transmitted rapidly and efficiently to such masses if chaos was to be averted. It was here that the telegraph came in. This invention allowed for the transmission of electrical impulses by cable over long distances, thanks to the use of the Morse Code system. Accordingly, huge armies could now be centrally controlled, concentrating rapidly on any nominated battle-field without confusion. As a result, the old intricate manoeuvres on the Enlightenment and Napoleonic pattern became less significant, as the telegraph could potentially warn any isolated force of a possible encirclement. The prospective victim could then retreat rapidly, especially if a convenient railway was close at hand. Accordingly, the Clausewitzian emphasis on battle became even more important, as Ardant du Picq appreciated:

> Battle has more importance than ever. Communication facilities such as the telegraph, concentration facilities such as the rail-way, render more difficult such strategic surprises as Ulm (1805) and Jena (1806). The whole forces of a country can thus be united. So united, defeat becomes irreparable, disorganisation greater and more rapid.
>
> Ardant du Picq (1880) 'Battle Studies' in *Roots of Strategy, Book 2*,
> Stackpole Books, 1987, p. 143.

The development of the railway and the telegraph therefore facil-itated the growth of large armies. They also had a profound effect upon the nature of military leadership. In essence, the combination of large forces and a complex railway network meant that planning had to be far more detailed: genius and intuition were no longer the essence of generalship. Armies now required a large, highly trained and well- organised body of staff officers, who could ensure that the troops reached their destination in good order. The importance of the staff corps was most graphically revealed during the Franco-Prussian War: the French, who neglected staff training and stressed battlefield courage, found themselves running around like the proverbial headless chickens; the Prussians, whose staff officers were regarded as the élite of their army, had no such problems and achieved a crushing victory as a result.

One by-product of the need for effective staff officers was the development of wargaming, which became a vital training tool – it served to identify officers of real talent. It was perhaps inevitable that the highly efficient Prussian army led the way. The first attempt came in 1824, when Lieutenant von Reisswitz devised his *kriegspiel*, which was the ancestor of all modern wargames, comprising as it did a rulebook, counters and a map. Civilian wargames have retained the von Reisswitz model (although many, like this book, now suggest the use of miniature figures on three-dimensional tabletop battlefields); however, the military eventually graduated to what was known as 'free *kriegspiel*'. This did not use a formal rulebook, but instead had an umpire adjudicating on the likely success or failure of the military manoeuvres suggested by the players. The 'free *kriegspiel*' approach proved to be an effective way of executing a highly flexible wargame: for a formal rulebook did not always cover all eventualities in the military context; a hopefully impartial umpire could, providing that he was extremely knowledgeable, conceive a feasible solution to a previously intractable difficulty. As a result, the 'free *kriegspiel*' is used by the military to this day as an essential training tool.

Industrialisation could therefore be seen to have made the deployment of most armies feasible; it also made a highly trained staff officer corps essential. However, armies would always meet their ultimate test on the battlefield – and the nineteenth century saw the mettle of officers and men face whole new dangers with the development of highly effective weapons.

THE REVOLUTION IN FIREPOWER
So far as infantry firearms were concerned, there was much room for improvement in 1815. The existing muzzle loading smoothbore

musket was, as has already been noted, extremely inaccurate: it was also distinctly prone to misfires. The latter problem was to a great extent solved by an improved firing mechanism known as the percussion cap; the former difficulty remained.

It had long been established that a rifled gun barrel would impart stability to a bullet through spinning it as it moved through the air. Unfortunately, existing military rifles could only function if the bullet fitted closely to the barrel. This necessitated physically ramming it down the muzzle, which required much greater effort than was the case with a smoothbore weapon, which in turn doubled the time taken to reload. However, the first half of the century saw the development of a bullet which expanded at the moment of firing: as a consequence, it no longer had to fit the barrel closely when loading. This solved the reloading problem at a stroke, which meant that whole armies could now be re-equipped with muzzle loading rifles. The effective firing range was at least doubled as a result.

This enhanced performance represented a significant improvement; a revolutionary change soon followed with the advent of breechloading rifles from the 1850s onwards. Breechloading technology had always been available, but there were serious difficulties involved in sealing the breech – and the consequent possibility of the rifle's blowing up in its user's face served as the ultimate argument against its adoption. However, industrialism saw the development of a fully sealed breech, and an infantry revolution followed. Soldiers could now fire three times more quickly than an enemy equipped with a muzzle loader; more importantly, breechloaders could be loaded and fired from a prone position, so that the soldier no longer presented such a conspicuous target. By the 1880s, rifles ceased to be single shot weapons but were instead loaded by magazines containing five rounds at a time; this further increased the potency of the infantryman.

Artillery was also to see significant improvements during the century. There had originally been a spirited conservative defence of the old muzzle loading smoothbore weapons, on the grounds that the short range canister ammunition (which consisted of packing a number of musket balls in a thin iron case which burst as it left the barrel upon firing: the effect was akin to a sawn-off shotgun) was more effective against infantry than the shells fired by the newfangled rifled guns. This was true as far as it went: unfortunately for traditionalists, the infantry rifle could now equal the range of canister ammunition, and inflict serious damage upon artillery in return. As a result, rifled cannon soon replaced the old smoothbores; the acquisition of steel rather than bronze barrels led to an additional increase in range, and the development of breechloading reduced the reloading time too.

All these ballistic improvements made the battlefield an even more hazardous place. Infantry were forced to respond by opening up their formations, for the old tightly packed columns, lines and squares represented an invitation to commit suicide. The new approach still used columns, but with the men keeping a slightly greater distance from their comrades. A portion of the formation was sent forward in dispersed formation to skirmish with the enemy; upon meeting significant resistance, additional men would be ordered to reinforce the skirmish line. These snipers would tend to broaden out, so that the effect was not unlike the old linear firing formation of Napoleonic times – with the difference that a reserve would always be deployed in columnar order, ready to charge a weakened and demoralised enemy.

This last point was fundamental: for all the improvements in the rifle and the increased prevalence of skirmishing, the final threat of the bayonet charge was generally what precipitated an enemy rout. In essence, the infantry objective remained what it always was since the invention of the musket – the enemy was to be routed by a bayonet charge, which would usually be preceded by a firefight.

THE DECLINE OF CAVALRY

The cavalry was proverbially the most conservative part of the army, being renowned for its social exclusivity and rejection of modernity. Accordingly, the increased lethality of firearms did nothing to alter the cavalry's belief in its utility. Horsemen conceded that the new infantry rifles presented something of an obstacle: they were however convinced that a preliminary bombardment from the new improved artillery would neutralise enemy infantry, thereby leaving the latter open to a successful charge. Rapid movement was held to be the unique quality of cavalry units, and was seen by writers such as du Picq to hold the key to success:

Rifled cannon and accurate rifles do not change cavalry tactics at all ... Accuracy of fire at a distance is impossible against a troop in movement, and movement is the essence of cavalry action.

Ardant du Picq (1880) 'Battle Studies' in *Roots of Strategy, Book 2,* Stackpole Books, 1987, p. 207.

This view of the efficacy of mounted troops was to prove hopelessly optimistic in the age of breech loading rifles. Quite simply, a cavalry charge needed to have too many factors in its favour if it was to succeed. It needed to enjoy prior artillery support; it required an approach largely undisturbed by enemy fire; and the charge had to target a demoralised or disorganised enemy unit: in essence, cavalry could be deterred from charging by a very limited amount of fire, given that horses are naturally predisposed to shy away from confronting solid obstacles (they prefer to either move around or jump over them). A volley of fire from an infantry unit equipped with smoothbore muskets would frequently deter a cavalry charge; it was scarcely surprising that a fusillade of more accurate, more rapid and longer range rifle fire would have a far more devastating effect.

Cavalry nevertheless persisted in believing in the efficacy of shock action. The occasional spectacular success, such as von Bredow's charge at the battle of Mars-la-Tour, was remembered; multiple failures were forgotten. Accordingly, cavalry leaders persisted in holding their forces in reserve, either waiting for a moment which never came, or squandering their men in an heroic yet futile charge.

All this was singularly unfortunate, for cavalry still had its uses. It could potentially have launched effective raids upon the enemy lines of communication, especially by targeting and tearing up railway tracks. It could also have performed its traditional reconnaissance duties by scouting enemy movements and preventing the enemy from doing the same; and on the battlefield, it could have eschewed its shock role, but instead have performed the role of mounted infantry, moving rapidly to key points and dismounting to fight. The last of these functions would have represented a revival of the original practice of the cavalry branch referred to as Dragoons – these had operated as mounted infantry in the seventeenth century, only to adopt a shock role during the eighteenth.

European cavalry largely rejected all these activities in the nineteenth-century continental wars (the colonial environment proved a different story). Only the Russian army utilised its dragoon units as mounted infantry, during the Russo-Turkish War. The only other types of cavalry resorting to raiding, scouting and dismounted action were irregular units such as the Russian Cossacks. As a result, enemy armies remained unscouted and their lines of communication left intact, as the cavalry was held in reserve waiting for the glorious charge that never came to pass.

TOWARDS ARMAGEDDON: THE MILITARISATION OF POLITICS

Bismarck's success in forging German unity on the back of Prussian military triumph led to the singularly dangerous belief that warfare was the answer to all social problems. European conservatives thought that socialist tendencies would always be neutralised if the future of the nation was held to be at stake. Moreover, they were partially correct in this analysis: the European working class proved distinctly bellicose at the onset of the First World War, promptly forgetting (with a few honourable exceptions) their ostensibly internationalist opposition to both capitalism and warfare.

This prevailing belief in the efficacy of warfare proved to be profoundly destabilising. It implied that, far from being subordinate to politics, military considerations dominated and indeed defined political objectives. This was especially true in Germany, which became a militarised society defined by the cult of the army. As a result, German politicians proved themselves willing to go to war without good reason, provided that their generals believed they could win. Other states followed this rather egregious example: Russian leaders felt that social agitation could be quelled by a crusade to liberate the Slavs from Ottoman rule; the Hapsburgs believed that a robust response to Balkan nationalism would win the respect of their own multinational Empire; and French reactionaries looked forward to the prospect of regaining Alsace and Lorraine from German control. In essence, Germany was all too often spoiling for a fight; and other nations were ready to meet the challenge.

Unfortunately, all the European states were convinced they would win any continental conflict. There was a general belief in the efficacy of the offensive. Du Picq gave expression to this prevailing view, arguing that the attacker would always gain the initiative, despite the destructive power of new weaponry:

With equal or even inferior power of destruction he will win who has the resolution to advance, who by his formations and manoeuvres can continually threaten his adversary with a new phase of material action, who, in a word has the moral ascendancy. Moral effect inspires fear. Fear must be changed to terror in order to vanquish.

> Ardant du Picq (1880) 'Battle Studies' in *Roots of Strategy, Book 2,*
> Stackpole Books, 1987, p 150.

This view proved ultimately to be misguided: it failed to account for the sheer destructive power of weaponry at the dawn of the twentieth century. In particular, the example of the American Civil War (1861–1865) was rejected. That conflict saw prolonged skirmishing duels between infantry units; the deployment of cavalry as a raiding force of mounted infantry; and a general absence of shock action. All these provided significant pointers for the future: however, European military thinkers like du Picq airily dismissed the American experience as being an affair of undisciplined amateurs:

The Americans have shown us what happens in modern battle to large armies without cohesion. With them the lack of discipline and organisation has had the inevitable results. Battle has been between hidden skirmishers, at long distance, and has lasted for days, until some faulty movement, perhaps a moral exhaustion, has caused one or other of the opposing forces to give way.

> Ardant du Picq (1880) 'Battle Studies' in *Roots of Strategy, Book 2,*
> Stackpole Books, 1987, p. 207.

It is all too easy to be critical of du Picq, (who was killed fighting for France during the Franco-Prussian War). He was undoubtedly correct to draw attention to the disorderly nature of American Civil War armies, the units of which displayed a tendency for rapid panic followed by equally speedy rallying: their lack of cohesion was inevitable in what were improvised forces. Du Picq was fully aware of the potential of modern weaponry, and penned *Battle Studies* as a response to the new order: he was moreover correct to assert that the determination of one army to assault its foe would invariably engender panic in the ranks of the latter. He simply failed to

21

appreciate the effects of the great improvements in modern weaponry, which crucially continued to intensify after his death.

The new military technology, combined with the ability of truly huge armies to present an unbroken line that could not be out-flanked, led to the slaughter of World War One. The nineteenth century had wrought a military revolution that was itself a product of the industrial age: the new social order led to seismic political change, which in turn led the monarchies to seek military solutions. Unfortunately for them, the same industrial civilisation inflicted such appalling attrition upon armed conflict that the old monarchies (Germany, the Hapsburg Empire, and Russia) would fall as a direct result of the very World War they were so willing to precipitate in 1914.

Chapter 2

Nineteenth-Century Wargaming

Wargaming is a difficult hobby to master. It requires a sound grasp of the respective capabilities of infantry, cavalry and artillery units, combined with an ability to exploit terrain features such as hills, woods, towns and roads. Faced with these problems, it makes a good deal of sense for any wargames rules writer to aim for simplicity in his or her design, thereby allowing the players to concentrate upon the game rather than spending all their time interpreting the rules.

There are those who object to this approach. Surely, they maintain, wargames rules should strive to cover all aspects of warfare: this is not only part of the quest for realism, but also strikes a blow for excellence, in contrast to the instant and utterly superficial pleasures of most hobbies today. The wargamer must and should, so the argument goes, aspire to the sort of intellectual credibility that can only be attained by playing games that are difficult to grasp and, by mastering such challenging products, acquire the respect of his or her peers.

This argument certainly has a good deal of facile validity; closer analysis does however refute it. For complex rules tend to suffer from conceptual flaws. The chief of these is what can be referred to as 'double jeopardy', or to be specific, accounting twice for a contingency that should only be considered once. For example, units which are behind cover frequently enjoy a morale bonus in complex rulesets: however, this fails to account for the fact that the role of cover has already been accounted for, given that the unit within would suffer fewer casualties than its more exposed comrades. If the unit behind cover is still suffering sufficient casualties to endure a morale test, then it is clear that the cover is no longer doing its job –

and should not therefore confer any morale bonus. Similarly, there is no reason to give special fighting abilities to élite units and penalties for unenthusiastic levies; these should already have been accounted for in the morale rules, which allow quality troops to carry on fighting for longer than a barely trained rabble (and inevitably inflicting far more damage in the process).

A lesser problem involves the perceived necessity of providing a good deal of technical minutiae with frequently marginal differences in weapons capabilities. This appears impressive, but is utterly pointless: rulesets should only deal with significant qualitative changes rather than minor performance shifts. In this way, the wargamer is made aware of decisive developments in weaponry, rather than drowning in peripheral detail.

The avowedly serious intent of complex rulesets tends to create further problems. The writers of such products are often very concerned to avoid any conceivable misinterpretation of their work. This is entirely understandable, but can result in rather convoluted prose more worthy of a parliamentary statute than what should be an entertaining hobby. Much of this stems from concerns over the machinations of those wargamers who have a tendency to exploit every conceivable textual loophole in order to win. Such players are exceptionally irritating: they do however only comprise a tiny minority of the hobby, and are best ignored. In essence, the quasi-legalistic approach to rules writing serves only to alienate potential players; moreover it fails to appreciate the distinction between laws (which are absolutely rigid edicts to be followed) and rules (which merely represent a guide to best practice). Accordingly, a set of wargames rules provides a statement of general intent: specific difficulties may arise, but are best resolved by friendly discussion between the players.

Simple rulesets are infinitely preferable to their more convoluted alternatives. They rely upon a great deal of prior analysis and interpretation, which is then distilled in a playable game. In so doing, essential detail is included, and peripheral irrelevancies removed. Designing a viable simple game is actually much more difficult than producing a complex product: the former has to identify only what is vital; the latter simply includes everything the writer knows.

The rules included within this book aspire to be both simple and realistic. The remainder of this chapter attempts to elucidate and expatiate upon the thinking behind my rules, which are contained in the next chapter; they can be referred to when necessary.

THE POST-NAPOLEONIC ETHOS

This book contains a single set of rules to cover the entire nineteenth century. Readers may find this curious, given the seismic changes in weaponry and their consequent effects upon the battlefield, as revealed in the previous chapter. One might argue that a plurality of rulesets would illustrate and amplify tactical shifts far more effectively than a single set.

The position outlined above certainly has a good deal of force; it does however fail to account for one very important consideration – specifically, the perceptions of the battlefield commanders themselves. The extent to which the latter continued to espouse such Napoleonic nostrums as infantry assaults in columnar formation preceded by skirmishers; the utility of a concentrated artillery barrage; and most notoriously, the continued efficacy of cavalry shock action, is striking. Any wargames designer should endeavour to create an appropriate mindset among the players: wargamers should always try to put themselves in the position of historical commanders, and think as their forebears did – and not project an anachronistic twenty-first century vision upon nineteenth-century practice. Nineteenth-century officers saw themselves operating in a post-Napoleonic environment; the use of a single ruleset to cover the entire century forces the same perceptions upon the wargamer.

Any historical wargame therefore involves a re-enactment of a plausible tactical situation. However, the historian (and all wargamers are necessarily historians) has another important duty: to reflect upon historical change and its effects. In this case, wargamers are examining how warfare developed during the nineteenth century. A single set of rules is especially valuable in this context: a direct comparison can be made between different types of weaponry along with the change of infantry formation from close to loose order.

In essence, the wargamer should both re-enact historical situations and reflect upon them. This twin objective is fraught with difficulty, given that it is sometimes hard to assess when role-playing should stop and analysis begin. It is however the key to good practice for the historian; and the use of a single ruleset to cover the entire period, is intended to facilitate the process.

UNITS AND FORMATIONS

I adopt an abstract approach to this area; giving a correct general impression is always far more important than drowning in petty minutiae. My units, for example, bear no relation to differing armies' Tables of Organisation and Equipment. Some might see this as a grievous failure, and an abdication of the designer's obligation to achieve absolute accuracy.

There are two reasons why I have adopted the approach of allocating a fixed general strength to all units of the same class. Firstly, the inaccuracy of any formal Table of Organisation and Equipment in practice: a couple of weeks of campaigning would see any unit afflicted by combat casualties, sickness and desertion – as a result, battlefield units could diverge quite widely from each other in terms of strength. Secondly, I work on the basis that a body of troops tends to act together: a given infantry grouping would occupy a finite area, and work towards the same goal. As a result, the group can for all practical purposes be treated as a single entity; whether or not it comprises two or three sub-units is an irrelevance.

This approach is designed to concentrate upon the practical effect of any design feature, rather than becoming enslaved by an inflexible and ultimately artificial process. Accordingly, unit types are divided into broad classes, the most important of which is the Infantry. This formed the core of all armies, and consists of four bases of figures. These march in columnar formation (depicted in four ranks of one base width) but fight in linear order (two ranks of two bases). The latter depicts either a formal line formation of two or three ranks; or where a large portion of the unit was sent ahead to skirmish with the enemy, with a reserve being deployed in column. The former approach was a feature of the first half of the century; the latter was adopted from the 1850s onwards. The practical effect was the same in each case: units marched towards the enemy in column formation, only to spread out if a firefight proved necessary. Accordingly, the respective formations can be depicted in the same way on the wargames table. The only significant distinction is to note the difference between the close order of the early century, and the looser approach adopted later. These have significant implications for both movement and combat.

The 'Skirmishers' classification is rather abstract. It is used to denote small groups of sharpshooters which historically added a little extra fire support to the main body of Infantry. They were extremely mobile, operating as they did in open order; they were also of low strength, which is why they only have two bases.

Nineteenth-century Cavalry units operated in line formation with a substantial portion in support to the rear: an alignment with two ranks of two bases depicts this rather well. Their entire *raison d'être* was the charge, which is why Cavalry units may not fire, even though they were frequently equipped with a firearm: they simply refused to use them to any significant extent. Readers with a Napoleonic background will doubtless be surprised that I have drawn no distinction between heavy cavalry and light horsemen: this is because nineteenth-century cavalry had an unfortunate tendency to neglect essential roles such as scouting and patrolling (previously the function of light horsemen), preferring instead to adopt the shock role that had represented the chief function of heavy cavalry units. Designations such as hussars, *chasseurs à cheval*, and cuirassiers may still have existed; they did however have no practical meaning.

Units of Dragoons can be depicted in the same formation as Cavalry (two ranks of two bases). This illustrates their marching order quite effectively; and also covers the appropriate area when a large portion of the unit dismounted to fire, and a small contingent held the horses. There is no need to use special dismounted figures, unless of course the wargamer wishes to invest in additional miniatures and spend time painting them – although it has to be said that the result will look splendid. Dragoon units may have played little role in European warfare during our period, but are included for their potential value: wargamers with a taste for exploring hypothetical possibilities, can test what could have happened if Dragoons had been deployed instead of Cavalry.

Artillery is always depicted by a single base with a gun and its crew. It is shown as being limbered for marching (with the gun barrel facing away from the enemy) or deployed for firing (with the barrel facing the enemy). Separate models of horses and limbers are not depicted, simply because to do so would result in the Artillery occupying too big an area, in relation to the other types of unit.

BASING AND SCALES

The rules provide suggestions on how many figures should be deployed on each base, together with the dimensions of the latter. All this information can be ignored: its main function is the purely aesthetic one of denoting different varieties of troops. It does allow the wargamer to distinguish between Infantry in close order and loose order; the difference between Infantry and Skirmishers; and to designate which mounted units are Cavalry and which are Dragoons. None of the information provided is essential – wargamers should use whichever basing system pleases them, and should certainly not feel compelled to waste time re-basing existing armies to fit in with the suggestions printed in my rules.

Readers may find this a rather casual attitude, and wonder in particular how on earth such an anarchic approach could possibly fit in with the scales used in the rules. The short answer is that this does not matter, because I do not use fixed scales in my wargames. Since this borders on the heretical for many wargamers, my rationale for this apparently singular decision requires an explanation.

The main reason for rejecting scales comes from the nature of the miniature wargames battlefield. In essence, the size of the figures is scarcely ever in a direct relationship with the terrain. The most obvious example can be seen in the case of the 28mm wargames miniature (which is usually closer to 30mm in practice). Let us postulate that the smallest significant hilltop would be around 60 feet in height. This would be 30cm on the wargames table; hills of such dimensions would dominate the landscape to such an extent as to look ridiculous. Similarly, trees scaled for 28mm figures are decidedly large, as are houses: many wargames are forced to resort to the convention that a town is represented by a single model of a dwelling. This is less of a problem with smaller figures: 6mm miniatures can provide a good compromise solution; but the only way of guaranteeing visual realism is to use 2mm figures. The latter have many virtues, but it must be said that they lack the visual splendour of larger miniatures. Any attempt to depict accurate scales will therefore have the unfortunate effect of negating the whole point of miniature wargaming – that is, the visual appeal of painted toy soldiers.

An even greater problem is presented when dealing with elapsed time. Wargames using fixed scales often calculate how far a reasonable move would be in relation to the size of the wargames table. They then calculate how long a unit would take to travel the requisite distance in reality, and construct a time scale from this. All this calculation sounds impressive. Unfortunately, the practical effects are a little odd. For example, many wargames rules work on the principle that 1cm equals 10 yards in reality – and that a move of 12cm is a reasonable move for an infantry unit. They calculate that this would represent 120 yards in reality: a unit would take about 2 minutes to march this far on the battlefield. Each wargames turn is therefore held to represent 2 minutes. However, most wargames battles are fought to a conclusion within 20 turns – or 40 minutes in terms of the time scale used. Most real battles took several hours to finish. The attempt to use accurate scales clearly led to farcical results in this example.

Many wargames designers simply ignore the problem of time, and retain their scale system whilst rejecting to address its problems. Others have acknowledged the dilemma and attempted to resolve it by means of a variable time scale. This postulates the concept of turns involving differing amounts of time lapse according to the activity being performed. For example, a turn consisting largely of artillery bombardment might be assumed to last one hour; whereas a cavalry charge might take just ten minutes. The late George Jeffrey did a good deal of very stimulating work in this area: however, he and his followers were unable to construct a clear or viable variable time wargame, for all their remarkable efforts. In essence, the concept was too flexible either for literary expression in a ruleset, or physical realisation on the wargames table.

In practice, the only way of allowing for the correct use of spatial and timing scales is to use gridded tables (either squares or hexagons), where each demarcated zone represents a given area. This eliminates the spatial problem by removing vertical scale from the equation; time difficulties can however remain, although the more rigid approach of grids does eliminate many problems – measurements will always be more precise when depicted by a clearly demarcated grid.

However, the best way to resolve the problems of scale is appropriately enough to adopt a nineteenth-century solution, and play 'free *kriegspiel*'. As the previous chapter described, this does not use miniature figures, but instead relies upon maps, with movement and combat regulated by an umpire. If the latter is truly an expert, a fascinating and rewarding game will result.

Miniature wargaming has advantages over such contrivances as grids and 'free *kriegspiel*', however. Chief among these is the visual beauty of painted miniatures and three dimensional tabletops. Playing a structural wargame or a 'free *kriegspiel*' can be a curiously bland experience: one can feel almost divorced from the action. Miniature wargaming in contrast effectively predicates direct involvement, for the tabletop general identifies closely with the army he or she has collected and painted. This experience of empathy is a vital part of realism, allowing wargamers to put themselves in the position of historical generals: wherever they see an enemy unit routed they feel the elation of victory; the sight of their own units being destroyed engenders all the anguish and humiliation of defeat. For this is not an abstract body of men represented by counters, or sketches on a piece of paper – these are the wargamer's very own little men. In this way, a miniature wargame can re-enact the historical experience in a manner very different, and infinitely superior to its physically anaemic 'free *kriegspiel*' rival.

The problems of scale do however remain. The best approach to miniature wargames design lies in recognising their intractability, by appreciating that any game using figures is an abstract construct. It relies upon a visually attractive synergy of troops and terrain, and an accurate interaction of movement, firing, and hand-to-hand combat in what is a created environment. This is done by evaluating how much fire any unit could be expected to endure in its approach march towards the enemy, and calculating movement distances and firing ranges from this. Similar abstractions apply with respect to time: one calculates how many moves are likely to be necessary in order to achieve a meaningful result, and declare this to be the length of the wargame. In both these cases, the game is intended to produce accurate practical effects, rather than be enslaved by the artificial process of fixed scales.

SEQUENCE OF PLAY

All my rulesets use a system of alternative turns, whereby one side completes charges, movement, and shooting, followed by a response from the other player. This may seem unrealistic; after all, it could be argued that everything should take place simultaneously, in order to reflect what happens on the real battlefield.

Unfortunately, simultaneity has its problems, both in terms of the mechanics and realism. Such systems tend to prove unworkable in practice, since with both players acting at the same time, there is a tendency for one player to glimpse what his or her opponent is up to with a particular unit. This is followed by a rather sneaky response to counter it. Rules designers tried to get round this problem by insisting that players wrote orders for each unit on every turn, before moving their armies. This had two serious defects. Firstly, writing orders for every unit took a long time; secondly, players tended to avoid their obligations by producing rather ambiguous suggestions hedged with qualifications. For example, instead of issuing an instruction to 'attack the Magdeburg woods' the edict would instead read 'attack the Magdeburg woods, unless the latter are garrisoned by two or more enemy units, or if an opportunity arises to take the opposing guard infantry in the flank'. Such orders tended to sabotage all the good intentions of the designer, and resulted in a great deal of bad feeling amongst players.

A more serious problem with a system of simultaneous turns, is its lack of realism. For it is only superficially true that everything that happens on the battlefield, occurs at the same time. Anyone who reads accounts of battles throughout history soon becomes aware of a distinctive pattern to such engagements: one general orders an attack, his enemy counters, the original attacker is forced to respond, and so on. This process is best reflected by a system of alternating turns, which can therefore be seen as more realistic and far less cumbersome, since written orders are not required.

It is however still important to reflect some aspects of enemy activity within one player's turn. Thus it is that any charge involves some firing from the defender, if the latter is equipped with firearms. Such firing involved fewer volleys than the number simulated in the normal sequence of events: however, the defender would be shooting at close range, where the effects are far more lethal. The defender must accordingly be given an opportunity to fire at any unit charging it; not to do so would be unrealistic.

CHANGES OF FORMATION

Many rulesets cover formation changes within the movement phase. I chose not to do so, for reasons both of utility and accuracy. It is simply much easier to allow units to change formation before they move, rather than go through the process of reducing a portion of their movement in order to perform the relevant evolution.

Some wargamers will doubtless be horrified at this apparently insouciant dismissal of a beloved tradition. However, the apparent oversimplification of my approach is actually more realistic than the traditional style, so far as the nineteenth century is concerned. This is because formation changes cover two specific types of units: Infantry and Artillery (evolutions of Dragoon and Skirmisher units occurred with such rapidity that they do not need separate consideration here). The alignments of these covered the two separate tasks of movement and firing. Artillery is a particularly straightforward case: it would move towards the enemy, reach an appropriate firing position and proceed to bombard the foe. Changing formation in a separate sequence before the movement phase ensures that Artillery may never fire on the same turn in which it moves – this covers the reality without unnecessary complications.

Infantry is a slightly different case, in that units in column formation may fire. This depicts those men who were sent ahead of the main body of the unit, and ordered to skirmish with the enemy. However, truly effective firing could only occur when the unit deployed in line formation – be that either the orthodox close order linear deployment of the early period, or the massed skirmishing in vogue towards the end of the century. In both cases, the decision to engage in a firefight involved the loss of forward movement. The elevation of changing formation to its own special part of the Sequence of Play serves to illustrate its significance on the battlefield: the decision to switch from movement to firing may have a salutary effect upon the enemy, but can also hand the initiative to the foe. Its vital significance on the wargames table is illustrated by giving changes of formation its own special place; wargamers will inevitably become aware of its importance as a result.

THE CHARGE SEQUENCE

A glance at the Charge Sequence section will show that there are detailed restrictions on when units may charge. The reader will for instance note that Skirmishers and Artillery units, who never engaged in hand-to-hand combat if they could possibly avoid it, may never charge. Conversely, all formed units may always engage Skirmishers and Artillery in mêlée; the best way for these to avoid damage is to keep their distance from enemy troops.

So far as mounted units are concerned, Cavalry may charge all units. This was after all the entire point of their existence. It should however be noted that the horsemen can suffer severely from defensive fire during their charge; this is very much in keeping with historical reality. As for units classified as Dragoons, these may never charge Cavalry: they would instead adopt a dismounted role, seeking to destroy the latter with small arms fire. They were however fully prepared to charge any other Dragoons and Infantry, to which they were measurably superior. This situation is best accounted for by allowing a charge to take place, but only if the aggressor has more bases remaining than the potential victim.

Similar considerations apply to Infantry, with the significant exception that they may never charge mounted units. For example, if they ever launched an attack upon a Dragoon unit, the latter would mount their horses and countercharge the Infantry – with distinctly sanguinary effects upon the men on foot. The rules are intended to show how both Infantry and Dragoons would usually engage in a firefight before charging, in order to establish a measurable superiority over the foe before resorting to close combat.

Readers should note that any charge will always proceed to a conclusion once embarked upon. Any last minute defensive fire could historically (and frequently did) inflict serious damage upon the aggressor, but would not actually prevent the charge from taking place: this must be reflected in any set of wargames rules.

MOVEMENT

Unit movement is depicted on a simple table, allowing instant reference. Readers should note that it is permissible to carefully measure all movement in advance. For example, the wargamer can quite legitimately ensure that his or her unit stops just outside the firing range of an enemy Infantry unit. This is because most historical unit leaders soon became fully aware of precisely how lethal each enemy firearm was, and calculated their movements accordingly.

Units can receive a considerable bonus to their movement rate if marching on a road, as might be expected. However, such movement entailed the reversion to a very deep formation of minimal width. There is no specific need to depict this physically, since the approach of any enemy unit would rapidly lead to the potential victim's switching back to combat formation. Units would simply never risk road movement in close proximity to the enemy: accordingly, they may not take advantage of a road if within 24cm of the foe. It should also be noted that units must start their turn on a road if they are to take advantage of it; forming into a marching column from battle order took some time to execute.

TURNING

Units turn by pivoting on their central point, for which a deduction may be levied on the standard movement rate. This is a good way of reflecting differences between formed Infantry and other units: the former can move quite rapidly if moving directly ahead in columnar formation, but will take some time to turn compared with Skirmishers or Cavalry.

Readers may look askance at my approach of executing turns by pivoting. This is because real nineteenth-century units realised turns by wheeling, whereby one corner of the unit remained stationary, whilst the opposite end marched the appropriate distance: once the entire unit had shifted alignment, it proceeded with its march. My approach therefore appears a flagrant violation of historical practice. However, one must always appreciate that a wargame is a created environment; the results must be replicated, but not necessarily the process by which the end is achieved. It is this context that explains and determines my use of pivoting, which ends at a stroke the more convoluted tradition of laboriously measuring a unit's outer wheeling distance. The practical effects of pivoting are identical to wheeling; the process is however much simpler, and it must be said more precise: measuring an outer corner's wheel accurately can be extremely difficult in practice.

34

FORMATION RESTRICTIONS

This section of the movement rules refers to Infantry and Artillery that are deployed for firing. In the case of Infantry units in linear formation, these may not move, but are permitted to turn in order to face a threat. This would however have a detrimental effect upon their firing capacity. Accordingly, Infantry that turns whilst in line formation may fire, but only with the effect of a unit deployed in column.

Artillery is never permitted to fire on the same move in which it turns. This looks rather odd on the face of it, given that the ordnance in question is depicted by a single model. That very base does however represent several guns, together with ammunition limbers and horses to tow the ordnance. Turning was in practice a rather complicated operation which cannot adequately be depicted on the wargames table; it must however be reflected in the firing rules, whereby Artillery may not fire in the same move in which it turns – the latter evolution would have allowed no time for a barrage.

MOVING AND FIRING

Most units are banned from firing as they advance. This is because any integral supporting fire would necessarily be greatly inferior to that of any adversary in a defensive position. If any unit wishes to advance without suffering undue casualties, its forward movement must be preceded by preparatory Artillery bombardment of enemy positions: wargamers who neglect this must and should suffer the consequences.

The only units that may combine firing with movement are Skirmishers. These were specifically trained not only to fire in the act of advancing, but also to take advantage of any available cover as they did so: in this way, the effect of firing from defending enemy units was minimised. Skirmishers may accordingly fire either before or after they move; they may as a result give active support to advancing or retreating friendly units – a tactic which any wargamer would be well advised to adopt.

INTERPENETRATION

Many wargames rules allow for units to pass through each other, providing additional stipulations to account for the endemic disorder created by the process. This tends to add a good deal of complexity to the rules. Such an approach is very satisfying for those who enjoy contemplating detailed rulebooks; it is however utterly redundant for practical purposes. It makes far more sense to simply ban interpretation in most cases: this forces the wargamer to organise his or her armies effectively and avoid traffic jams.

Skirmisher units are unaffected by the above stipulations, and may interpenetrate freely. This depicts the historical situation whereby small groups of men in open formation could easily move through or around other units.

FIRING

The simulation of fire combat is a great challenge for any rules writer covering nineteenth-century Europe. He or she has to deal both with a multiplicity of constantly improving weaponry, and a variety of target formations. The core procedure adopted here is similar to that used in my previous books: a number of dice are rolled for each base firing, which in turn inflict hits upon the enemy; and when four hits are accrued, a base is removed from the target unit (totals under four are logged and carried over until the victim is engaged again).

Any viable set of wargames rules must simulate an accurate synergy between fire and movement: the precise extent of firing a unit would have to endure whilst approaching the enemy should be calculated, and the effective weapon ranges extrapolated from this. The latter is key: there was always a great difference between any weapon's theoretical maximum range, and the point at which the target received significant damage. The stress of battle would lead to hurried firing; being shot at would exacerbate tension and affect accuracy; the lack of smokeless gunpowder (which was only brought into service at the end of the century) meant that the target tended to be enveloped in a fine mist; and the potential victim could always take advantage of uneven terrain, since few battlefields were ever completely flat.

The precise number of dice rolled for each base firing is determined by two factors: accuracy and the rate of fire. The former is usually accounted for by the range of the weapon; in the case of artillery however, it also became a factor with the effectiveness of the barrage. Thus it was that rifled artillery with steel barrels not only had a longer effective range than other types, but was also more accurate than its inferior rivals at all ranges – with the exception of smoothbore artillery firing canister ammunition in close proximity to the enemy. Rate of fire became an exceptionally important consideration with breechloading small arms.

Each die needs to achieve a particular score in order to register a hit. This is affected both by the type of firing unit and the formation of the target. The former consideration takes account of the number of men firing. For example, Skirmisher units may have consisted of marksmen (which is why they are assigned a longer range than Infantry with the same weapons), but they had very few soldiers in their ranks – for this reason, their fire is less effective than Infantry in line formation. So far as the target is concerned, its deployment has significant consequences for the effectiveness of any firing directed against it. This is why Cavalry is especially vulnerable, representing as it does a large and tightly-packed target; the more dispersed loose order Infantry is much less likely to suffer damage.

Flexible though the firing tables are, they cannot cover all possible contingencies. It is here that the concept of the 'saving roll' comes to the rescue. This idea was introduced by the great miniature wargame pioneer Donald Featherstone, who can be described as the father of the hobby – without him and his outstanding work, tabletop wargaming would be in a much poorer state. The saving roll works on the principle that for every hit inflicted, a die is rolled on behalf of the target; and if the relevant saving roll is achieved, the potential hit fails to take effect. In these rules, the saving roll is allocated to units in cover, and those equipped with breechloading weapons. It will be recalled that these could be loaded and fired from a prone position; since this inevitably led to fewer casualties than those unfortunates who had to stand up when operating their muzzleloading small arms, men equipped with breechloaders enjoy the benefits of an enhanced saving roll. This even applies to Infantry in columnar array: the main body may have been standing up, but the advanced force of skirmishers would (if equipped with breech-loading weapons) have been in a prone position.

HAND-TO-HAND COMBAT

The procedure for mêlée is similar to that for firing, in that a number of dice are rolled for each base engaged in combat. The significant difference is that the defender is always allowed to fight back simultaneously; this simulates either the crossing of bayonets, or firing at point-blank range.

The number of dice rolled is dependent upon who is fighting whom. For example, a clash between two Cavalry units tended to be absolutely equal, so that one die is rolled for each base engaged; in the case of Cavalry engaging Skirmishers however, a decidedly unequal contest would ensue: in consequence, four dice are rolled for each base of horsemen involved, and only one for the men on foot.

Readers will note that Cavalry suffers a reduction in combat power when fighting Infantry in close order. This is intended to illustrate the difference in clashes between Cavalry and Infantry throughout the nineteenth century. The first half saw foot soldiers equipped with muskets, whose fire could not always be relied upon to drive off attacking horsemen, owing to its very short effective range. As a consequence, Infantry adopted close order formation, which presented a serious obstacle to a Cavalry attack, given the unwillingness of horses to attack a major barrier. This was especially true when the foot soldiers were deployed in column formation; for the latter could easily switch to the even more formidable square which, by presenting an obstacle that could not be outflanked, was an especially daunting target for Cavalry units. There is no specific need to provide rules for square formation: its temporary use in extremis is already accounted for, by making close order columns very formidable when defending against Cavalry attack. As for the second half of the nineteenth century, the improved Infantry fire-arms were likely to stop a mounted assault by themselves: consequently, they adopted a loose order formation to enhance mobility and reduce casualties from enemy fire. This may have made them vulnerable to Cavalry that were able to engage them in mêlée; that however was becoming an increasingly rare event.

Additional dice are provided for such events as a flank attack, or defending a hilltop or a river. Readers may wonder why units defending woods or towns do not receive extra dice, but instead only have a saving roll. This is due to the specific nature of such engagements, which only ever involved assaults by Infantry units. In these cases, the key problem was summoning up the nerve to charge in the first place (covered by the rule that Infantry may only attack its enemy counterpart, if the charging unit is of superior strength at the start of the Charge Sequence). Once the charge was launched, the defender would always be at something of a moral disadvantage: the cover provided by a wood or a town would however serve to blunt the enemy charge to some extent, which is why a saving roll is more appropriate for the defender to enjoy than a combat bonus.

RETREATS

The side that loses the greatest number of casualties in the mêlée itself (losses from defensive fire are not covered in this calculation, since these happened before the hand-to-hand combat occurred) must retreat – and in a tied result, the defender must always withdraw. This is intended to reward the attacker for seizing the initiative in a manner befitting the aggressive nature of post-Napoleonic doctrine: it also enacts the trauma of being on the receiving end of a charge.

MORALE

This aspect of warfare is possibly the most significant of all – a point reinforced by Napoleon's utterance that the moral was three times as important as the physical. As a result, many wargame designers felt compelled to write some very complex rules, accounting for every conceivable aspect of morale.

Rules that relied upon complexity often demanded that morale be assessed for a wide range of reasons. Typical occasions were: when declaring a charge; when receiving a charge; when fired at during a charge; when shot at for the first time; if engaged in the flank or rear; when first reaching losses of 50 per cent; and if suffering 20 per cent or greater casualties in a single engagement. Nor did the complexity stop there. When testing morale, units would have to account for such factors as the proximity of friendly and enemy units; how well the testing unit was supported; the formation status of the unit; its current state of disorder; its strength at the start of the move; the casualties lost this turn; and the number of hand-to-hand combats the unit had won or lost during the game. After all this was evaluated, the range of results had to be considered. Units could pass their test; they could be unformed; they could be disordered;

they could retire one move; retreat two moves; rout until they were rallied; or they could surrender.

All this sounds very impressive, and exceptionally realistic. Such appearances are singularly deceptive: realism is entirely lacking, despite the detail. In essence, rules of this ilk simply fail to consider the precise nature of losing morale. Instead of wasting time taking morale tests for peripheral reasons, wargames rules should only call a unit's state of well-being into question when suffering serious potential trauma. This occurred on three occasions in the nineteenth-century context. The first of these was whenever significant damage had been inflicted by enemy fire, simulated here by the removal of a base. Secondly, Cavalry units could suffer extreme disorder if shot at in the process of charging, even if the fire did not cause significant material damage (in cases where both the above contingencies apply, the unfortunate unit must take two morale tests). Finally, units which lost a round of hand-to-hand combat could suffer especially severe trauma; this is simulated by taking two morale tests at the conclusion of their mandatory retreat. It should be noted that the victors of any mêlée never have to test morale, even if they lose a base in the process: the euphoria of success would always overcome the trauma of any losses suffered in achieving it.

Since the number of reasons for assessing morale have been reduced so drastically, the test mechanism can also be simplified, since a true crisis is being simulated. Accordingly, a die is rolled, with an additional base being removed if the relevant score (which varies according to the quality of the unit) is not achieved. This allows for such factors as retreats, routs, disorder, and anything else leading to a reduction in combat capacity, with none of the complication of having to keep different records for each unit.

The system is intended to reflect the true effects of loss of morale. Specifically, this was a diminution of combat effectiveness. This is also the best way to reward élite units, and penalise levies. By being more likely to pass their tests, higher quality units will remain intact for longer (by not losing so many bases) and perform more effectively as a result. As a consequence, élite units are not given extra bonuses for their combat performance: this has already been accounted for in the morale rules – and as I have frequently stated in this chapter, units should never be rewarded or penalised twice for the same contingency.

It should be noted that Artillery units, consisting as they do of just one base, never have to test morale. This reflects their historical situation: gunners would always carry on firing until they and their ordnance were shattered by enemy fire, or destroyed in hand-to-hand combat. There is no need for separate morale tests.

LEADERSHIP

Many contemporary sets of wargames rules include detailed provisions for command and control; it represents an especially prevalent fashion – and like most trends, it tends to be followed without question. I have always wondered whether any special stipulations are essential: any wargamer is fully capable of making many mistakes without the added burden of leadership restrictions – the tension of the wargames battlefield can realistically invoke the requisite qualities of doubt, indecision or brilliance. Accordingly, there is no need to insert compulsory command rules.

Leadership rules can add a new dimension to wargaming, however. I have accordingly provided optional insertions where relevant. These are predicated upon the notion of restricting (or occasionally enhancing) movement rates and combat capabilities. This is designed to reflect the nineteenth-century battlefield, which was becoming increasingly larger with the passage of time – and a bigger area meant less opportunity to control all the army's units as the commanding general might have wished.

The leadership rules provided with each scenario can enhance the wargaming experience. They are however far from essential – enjoyable, fulfilling and realistic games will always occur without them. As with any optional rules, they should only be included if both players agree to their use.

Chapter 3

Nineteenth-Century Wargames Rules

UNITS AND FORMATIONS

(a) *Infantry.* Units have four bases, which operate in either close or loose order. They may adopt the following formations:

    (i) *Line.* Comprising two ranks of two bases.

    (ii) *Column.* Comprising four ranks of one base.

(b) *Skirmishers.* Units have two bases which deploy in a single rank.

(c) *Cavalry and Dragoons.* Units have four bases. They deploy in two ranks of two bases.

(d) *Artillery.* These consist of a gun and four crew on a single base. Guns are either limbered (denoted by turning the barrel away from the enemy) or deployed (barrel facing the enemy).

BASING

The details provided below are merely suggestions – there is absolutely no need to re-base existing wargames armies in order to use these rules.

(i) *Base Widths*

	Figure Size				
	2–6mm	10–15mm	20–25mm	28–30mm	40–42mm
Base Width	30mm	40mm	60mm	80mm	100mm

(ii) *Figures per Base*

Troop Type	Figures per Base
Infantry (Close Order)	4
Infantry (Loose Order), Cavalry	3

| Skirmishers, Dragoons | 2 |
| Artillery | 1 Gun and 4 Crew |

HOW TO WIN
Victory conditions are determined by the battle scenario being played. Consult the relevant chapters for details.

SEQUENCE OF PLAY
Each complete turn comprises two player turns. Each wargamer follows the sequence listed below in his or her player turn:

(1) Changes of Formation.
(2) The Charge Sequence.
(3) Movement
(4) Firing.
(5) Hand-to-Hand Combat.

(1) Changes of Formation
(1a) *Relevant units.* Only Infantry and Artillery units may change formations.

   (i) Infantry may change from Column to Line or vice versa. They remain facing in the original direction.

   (ii) Artillery may change from Limbered to Deployed or vice versa.

(1b) *Penalties.* Changing formation *per se* has no effect on a unit's ability to move or fire.

(2) The Charge Sequence
Units that wish to charge proceed according to the following sequence:

(2a) *Check Restrictions.* Check the following table to see if a charge may take place.

Charging Unit	Cavalry	Dragoons	Infantry	Skirmishers	Artillery
Cavalry	Yes	Yes	Yes	Yes	Yes
Dragoons	No	Conditional	Conditional	Yes	Yes
Infantry	No	No	Conditional	Yes	Yes
Skirmishers and Artillery	No	No	No	No	No

(i) *Conditional Charges.* These may only take place if the pro-spective charging unit begins the Charge Sequence with more bases than its potential victim.

(2b) *Measure the distance between attackers and defenders.* If this exceeds the attacker's eligible move, then the charge does not take place and the rest of this sequence is ignored.

(i) Only one unit may charge each face of the defending unit (these being front, left flank, right flank, and rear).

(ii) A charging unit may only turn once; this evolution may not exceed 45°.

(2c) *Defenders fire.* If a charge takes place against the front face of a defending unit, then the latter may fire against their assailants before contact.

(i) *Short-ranged weapons.* Defending units equipped with mus-kets may still fire at their aggressors, even if the latter com-mence their charge beyond the range of the defenders' weapons.

(2d) *Move the charging unit into contact.* Resolve all fighting in the Hand-to-Hand Combat phase.

(3) MOVEMENT

(3a) *Movement table.* Cross reference the unit type with the relevant terrain to find the movement distance. Reduce this by the appropriate fraction each time the unit turns. Each turn can be of any amount.

		Terrain			
Unit	Open	Woods or Towns	Crossing Streams	Road	Deduction per Turn
Infantry (loose order)	12	8	8	16	¼
Infantry (close order)	8	4	4	16	¼
Skirmishers	12	12	12	16	No deduction
Cavalry and Dragoons	16	May not enter	12	24	No deduction
Artillery	12	May not enter	May not cross	16	No deduction

(3b) *Bridges.* These negate the effect of streams. Units which cross a bridge are treated as being in open terrain or on a road (see **3c** below).

(3c) *Roads.* Units may use the road movement rate if the following conditions apply:

(i) They spend their entire turn on the road.

(ii) They do not move within 24cm of an enemy unit.

(3d) *Towns.* Only one unit can normally occupy a town, but very large towns may hold more. For example, see the Battle of Kissingen scenario; Chapter 14 and Map 10.

(3e) *Turning.* Units turn by pivoting on their central point.

(i) Units moving by road are never penalised for turning.

(3f) *Formation Restrictions: Infantry.* Infantry in Line formation has the following limitations:

(i) It may not move, and therefore cannot charge.

(ii) It may turn freely.

(iii) It may fire after turning, but only with the effectiveness of a unit in Column formation.

(3g) *Formation Restrictions: Artillery.* Deployed Artillery has the following limitations:

(i) It may not move.

(ii) It may turn freely.

(iii) It may not fire after turning.

(3h) *Moving and Firing.* Only Skirmishers may combine firing with movement. They may fire either before or after they move.

(3i) *Interpenetration.* Skirmishers may pass through friendly units freely.

(i) Other units may not; they are eliminated if forced to do so by a retreat following Hand-to-Hand Combat.

(4) Firing

The procedure for firing is as follows:

(4a) *Adjudge field of fire.* Units may only fire at any single target within 45° of their frontal facing.

(i) Units defending towns. These have a field of fire of 360° and all of the unit can fire in any direction.

(4b) *Observation.* Firing units must have a line of sight to their targets. This may be blocked by obstructions.

(i) *Obstructions.* Woods, Towns, Hills and other units are all treated as obstructions.

(ii) *Firing at the same level.* The line of sight is always blocked by any obstruction on the same elevation as the firing unit.

(iii) *Firing from hills to ground level.* The line of sight is only blocked if the obstruction is closer to the target unit than the firing unit.

(iv) *Firing from ground level to hills.* The line of sight is only blocked if the obstruction is closer to the firing unit than the target.

(4c) *Measure range.* Consult the following table to see if the firing unit can shoot:

Weapon	Range
Steel Rifled Artillery	60cm
Bronze Rifled Artillery	48cm
Smoothbore Artillery	32cm
Later Breechloading Rifle	24cm
Early Breechloading Rifle, Rifled Musket	16cm
Smoothbore Musket	8cm

(i) *Skirmishing bonus.* Units of Skirmishers always add 8cm to the weapon ranges given above.

(ii) *Canister ammunition.* Smoothbore Artillery units fire with greater accuracy at short range (0–12cm).

(4d) *Collect dice.* An examination of the following table will reveal how many dice are rolled for each base in the firing unit:

Weapon	Dice per Base
Smoothbore Artillery (short range)	5
Steel Rifled Artillery	4
Bronze Rifled Artillery	3
Smoothbore Artillery (long range), Breechloading Rifles	2
Muskets	1

(4e) *Roll dice.* For every die that achieves the relevant score on the table below, a hit is registered on the target unit:

Firing Unit	Defending Unit Class A	B	C	D
Infantry (Line formation), Artillery	2–6	3–6	4–6	5–6
Skirmishers, Dragoons	3–6	4–6	5–6	6
Infantry (Column formation)	4–6	5–6	6	6

46

(i) The defending unit's class is defined below:

Unit Class	Unit Type
A	Cavalry
B	Infantry in Close Order (Column formation)
C	Dragoons, Artillery (Limbered),
	Infantry in Loose Order (Column formation),
	Infantry in Close Order (Line formation)
D	Skirmishers, Artillery (Deployed),
	Infantry in Loose Order (Line formation)

(4f) *Saving Rolls.* The defending unit rolls a die for every hit that has been registered. For each saving roll achieved, the hit does not take effect.

(i) Saving Roll Table

	Unit Defence Class		
Unit Location	**1**	**2**	**3**
Woods or Towns	3–6	4–6	5–6
Open Terrain	5–6	6	No Save

(ii) The unit's class is defined below:

Defence Class	Unit Type
1	Infantry (Line formation; Breechloading weapons); Skirmishers (Breechloading weapons).
2	Infantry (Column formation; Breechloading weapons); Dragoons (Breechloading weapons).
3	Infantry, Skirmishers and Dragoons (Muzzleloading weapons); Cavalry; Artillery.

(4g) *Log Remaining Hits.* For every four hits acquired, a base is removed from the defending unit (if under four hits remain, carry the total over until the next combat is resolved).

(5) Hand-to-Hand Combat

Hand-to-Hand Combat is always simultaneous, with both sides attempting to inflict casualties upon each other. The procedure is as follows:

(5a) *Collect Dice.* A variable number of dice are rolled for each base remaining in the unit. To ascertain how many dice each base should roll, cross-reference one's own unit type with that of the enemy:

			Enemy Unit		
Own Unit	Cavalry	Dragoons	Infantry (Column formation)	Infantry (Line formation)	Skirmishers, Artillery
Cavalry	1	2	2	3	4
Dragoons (Charging)	–	2	2	2	3
Dragoons (Defending)	1	1	–	–	–
Infantry (Charging)	–	–	2	2	3
Infantry (Defending)	1	1	1	–	–
Artillery	1	1	1	1	–

- **(i)** *Additional dice.* Units roll one additional die per base for each of the following that apply: (a) attacking enemy flank or rear (not when attacking units in towns); (b) defending riverbank against attackers who are crossing the river in order to engage them frontally; and (c) on higher ground than opponent.
- **(ii)** *Reduced dice.* Cavalry units roll one fewer die per base if engaging enemy Infantry units in close order.

(5b) *Roll Dice.* Hits are registered for each roll of 4–6.

(5c) *Saving Rolls.* Defending units in Woods or Towns receive a saving roll of 5–6 for every potential hit.

(5d) *Log Remaining Hits.* This procedure is identical to that detailed in the Firing section (see rule 4g).

(5e) *Loser Retreats.* The unit which has taken the greatest number of hits in the hand-to-hand combat must retreat 12cm. It faces the enemy at the end of its withdrawal.
- **(i)** *Blocked Retreat.* As already stated in the rules for Interpenetration (rule 3h), only Skirmishers may retreat through friendly units. Other units are eliminated if forced to do so.
- **(ii)** *Ties.* If the scores are level after a hand-to-hand combat, the defender retreats.

(iii) *Automatic Elimination.* Artillery units may not retreat if they lose a hand-to-hand combat, and are instead eliminated.

(5f) *Multiple Aggressors.* In cases where a plurality of attacking units are engaged in hand-to-hand combat, the defending unit may only inflict casualties upon the unit attacking its frontal face.

(5g) *Retreat from Towns.* If the defending unit retreats from a town, the attacking unit may instantly take its place.

(6) Morale

(6a) *Testing Morale.* A unit must test morale under the following circumstances, at the instant they occur:

(i) For every base removed from the unit this turn, as a result of enemy firing (test once per base removed).

(ii) It is a charging Cavalry unit that is shot at by its potential victim (test once).

(iii) It has lost a hand-to-hand combat this turn (two morale tests are required for this condition).

(6b) *Morale Procedure.* For each mandated test, roll a die and consult the table below. If the unit fails to achieve the score required, remove a complete base:

Unit Class	Die Roll Required
Fanatic	2–6
Elite	3–6
Average	4–6
Levy	5–6
Rabble	6

Chapter 4

Wargames Scenarios

Warfare in real life is notoriously unpredictable. Plans are all too apt to go awry as units become delayed; or they become bogged down on inadequate roads; or subordinate generals misinterpret their orders. So many things could go wrong in reality, and frequently did.

In contrast to this rather chaotic picture, too many wargames are both rigidly structured and decidedly predictable. Many rule-sets provide points systems where units are rated for their competence, so that a poorly-armed rabble would be worth one tenth of the value of (for example) a Guards infantry regiment. The idea is that games should always be fought between two armies of equal points values – a concept of such palpable absurdity that it almost defies description. This distinctly singular approach to simulating warfare is invariably compounded in wargames competitions: these not only espouse the aforementioned principle of contrived equality, but exacerbate the situation by allowing encounters between armies which could never conceivably have fought each other historically.

The scenarios proposed in this chapter adopt a very different approach. For a start, there is no points system; armies start the gaming process with an identical number of units. This device has been adopted in all my previous books, and is intended to depict the overall combat power of particular armies – and also the important fact that generals would never accept the offer of a battle from an antagonist who enjoyed massive numerical superiority: a commander would only fight historically if he thought his army was strong enough to defeat the foe, which is why opposing armies tended to be of similar size in battles. They were not unfortunately always of the same quality; it has to be said that history was not always fair – a situation that must be reflected on the wargames table, where some armies will be superior to their foes. This situation is graphically illustrated in the next chapter, which provides a selection of army lists detailing the armament, morale status, and specific tactical restrictions that affect different nations.

Many things could however go wrong before the battle even started, as was outlined in the first paragraph of this chapter. Accordingly, each scenario included has a pre-battle phase, with results that vary from allowing a potentially decisive flank attack, to units never arriving on the battlefield at all. In this way the wargamer is forced to adapt to unforeseen circumstances; this may be frustrating, but is also realistic – and once again, irritatingly but accurately unfair. Should the wargames generals find themselves on the receiving end of an unfavourable set of circumstances, they can console themselves with the thought that overcoming vicissitudes of ill-fortune is the ultimate test of any leader, and that here is an opportunity to test their mettle.

I have provided two suggested table layouts for my scenarios: one to cover the normal sized battles fought on a table of 120cm × 90cm (scenarios 1–4), and one for the small encounters featured in the minigame fought over an area of 60cm × 60cm (scenario 5). The maps have been divided into squares to facilitate their re-creation; each square represents an area of 30cm × 30cm. Readers can of course design their own terrain layouts as desired: the only proviso is that normal battles should have three objectives to be seized, and minigames should have two.

SCENARIO 1: PITCHED BATTLE

This scenario has the classic situation whereby both generals are ready, willing and able to accept battle. As has already been outlined however, things may not go quite the way that either side intends.

(1) *How to win.* Two out of the three objectives must be occupied by the end of Game Turn 15 (a Game Turn consists of two player turns; one for the Attacker and one for the Defender).

(2) *Army Selection.* Generals seldom had the luxury of being able to choose the number and type of units for their armies. Accordingly, each wargamer rolls a die and consults the table

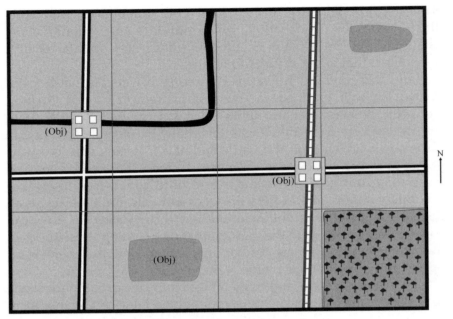

Map 1. A Suggested Battlefield: Scenarios 1–4

below, in order to ascertain the precise constitution of his or her army.

Unit Type

Die Roll	Infantry	Skirmishers	Cavalry	Artillery
1	4	1	3	2
2	4	2	2	2
3	5	1	2	2
4	5	2	1	2
5	5	1	1	3
6	6	1	1	2

(3) *Determining Sides.* Both players roll a die. The one who rolls highest decides whether he or she wishes to be the Attacker or the Defender.

(4) *Deployment Area.* The Defender rolls a die to determine which table edge will form his or her baseline (the Attacker naturally has the opposite edge as his or her base).

Die Roll	Baseline Edge
1–2	North
3–4	South
5	West
6	East

(5) *Pre-Battle Events.* Both players roll a die, and act according to the results indicated.

Die Roll	Event
1–2	Bogged Down
3–4	Traffic Congestion
5–6	Flank March (Attacker)
	Forward Deployment (Defender)

(a) *Bogged Down.* Two units from the starting force have become irretrievably delayed on appalling roads, and do not arrive on the battlefield. At least one of these eliminated units must be Artillery.

(b) *Traffic Congestion.* Three units (at least one must be Infantry) have been delayed during the chaotic march to the battlefield. The general rolls another die: the late arrivals appear anywhere on the friendly baseline on the relevant turn.

Die Roll	Turn
1–2	4
3–4	5
5–6	6

(c) *Flank March.* Three of the attacker's units (at least one of which must be Cavalry and none of which may be Artillery) appear on either enemy flank: the Attacking general chooses which at the start of the game. The Attacker rolls a die to determine the turn on which the flanking force arrives.

Die Roll	Turn
1–2	4
3–4	5
5–6	6

(d) *Forward Deployment.* Three Defending units (none of which may be Artillery) may deploy in advance of the rest of the army. The distance each unit may deploy ahead of its baseline is stated below:

Unit	Distance from Baseline
Infantry	15–30cm
Skirmishers, Cavalry	15–45cm
Dragoons	15–60cm

(6) *Defender Deploys Army.* The defending general deploys his or her army within 15cm of its baseline (apart from units affected by Pre-Battle Events).

(7) *Attacker Deploys Army.* The attacking general deploys his or her army within 15cm of its baseline (apart from units affected by Pre-Battle Events).

(8) *Begin the Game.* The Attacker always goes first in every Game Turn.

SCENARIO 2: MEETING ENGAGEMENT

This scenario simulates the rare but not unprecedented historical occasions where two enemy armies are unaware of each other's proximity and blunder into contact. The resulting battles always tended to be very chaotic and utterly unpredictable.

(1) *How to Win.* See Pitched Battle Scenario.

(2) *Army Selection.* See Pitched Battle Scenario.

(3) *Determining Sides.* See Pitched Battle Scenario.

(4) *Deployment Area.* See Pitched Battle Scenario.

(5) *Select On-Table Forces.* This scenario postulates that a pair of enemy contingents see each other on the battlefield and send a courier to the commanding general for reinforcements. These initial forces comprise three units: one must be Infantry; one must be Cavalry; and one must be a Reconnaissance unit (either Skirmishers or Dragoons). Any relevant units from the Army List may be selected.

(6) *Defender Deploys On-Table Forces.* Infantry and Cavalry deploy within 15cm of their baseline; the Reconnaissance unit sets up between 15cm and 45cm from its baseline.

(7) *Attacker Deploys On-Table Forces.* The initial Attacking force is set up according to the same criteria as for the Defender.

(8) *Select Marching Columns.* The ten units in each army are divided into Marching Columns (each of which comprises two units).

(9) *Determine March Order.* Each general decides the order in which the Marching Columns will arrive on the battlefield (no more than one Column will appear in any one player's turn).

(10) *Begin the Game.* The Attacker always goes first in each Game Turn.

> **(a)** *Dicing for Marching Columns.* Each player rolls a die at the start of each of their Movement phases. On a roll of 4–6, the next available Marching Column arrives anywhere on the friendly baseline.

SCENARIO 3: REARGUARD ACTION

Paradoxical as it may seem, the most crucial moment of any battle occurred after it was over. To be specific, all the bloodshed could prove pointless unless the victorious general led a vigorous pursuit of the vanquished; this was essential if a defeat was to be turned into a rout. This scenario assumes that the victor of a battle is trying to sweep aside an enemy rearguard. If successful, the entire enemy army is assumed to be effectively annihilated; failure will result in the foe making a tactical retreat rather than a precipitate rout.

(1) *How to Win.* The Attacker must exit at least five units off the Defender's baseline by the end of Turn 15 (note that this is the only scenario in which any side may voluntarily order its units to leave the table).

> **(a)** Units that exit the table voluntarily may never return in subsequent turns.
>
> **(b)** Attacking units that retreat off the table as a result of losing a hand-to-hand combat are eliminated: they do not count as having exited the table voluntarily.

(2) *Determining Sides.* Both players roll a die, with the winner deciding on whether he or she wishes to Attack or Defend.

(3) *Deployment Area.* The Defender rolls a die to determine which table edge will form his or her baseline (the Attacker naturally has the opposite edge as his or her base).

Die Roll	Baseline Edge
1–3	West
4–6	East

(4) *Defender Selects Army*. The Defending general chooses his or her army by rolling a die and consulting the following table: the result indicates the numbers of each unit type he or she deploys.

Unit Type

Die Roll	Infantry	Skirmishers	Cavalry	Artillery
1	3	1	1	0
2	3	0	1	1
3	2	1	1	1
4	2	0	1	2
5	2	0	2	1
6	2	1	2	0

(5) *Attacker Selects Army*. The Attacking general selects his or her army by rolling a die and consulting the Army Selection Table for the Pitched Battle Scenario (scenario 1, section 2).

(6) *Attacker Divides Army*. The victorious Attacking army is assumed to be pursuing the foe in an exhilarated but slightly disordered condition. As a consequence, the army will not arrive as a cohesive whole. The following procedure is adopted:

(a) The Attacker selects a starting force of four units. These enter the game on Turn 1.

(b) The remaining Attacking units are divided into three groups of two units. These enter the game in sequence (no more than one group per turn) from Turn 2 onwards.

(7) *Defender Deploys Army*. All defending units are set up within 90cm of the relevant baseline.

(8) *Begin the Game*. The Attacker takes the first turn in each Game Turn.

(a) The Attacker's starting force enters the game on Turn 1.

(b) The Attacker rolls a die at the start of each Attacking Movement Phase from Turn 2 onwards. On a roll of 3–6 the next available Attacking group will arrive on the table.

SCENARIO 4: FLANK ATTACK

A flank attack represented the apogee of military excellence. It was frequently attempted but not always successfully consummated. This scenario gives wargamers the chance to execute it. The Attacker is assumed to have distracted the Defender's attention with a small portion of the aggressor's army, whilst the remainder will put in a spectacularly unwelcome appearance on the putative victim's flank.

(1) *How to Win.* The Attacker must control all three objectives by the end of Turn 15. Failure to do so results in victory for the Defender.

(2) *Determining Sides.* Both players roll a die, with the winner deciding on whether he or she wishes to Attack or Defend.

(3) *Attacker Deploys Pinning Force.* The Attacking general sets up one Infantry unit, one Cavalry unit and one Artillery unit within 15cm of the northern edge of the table.

(4) *Defender Selects Army.* The Defender selects his or her army by rolling a die and consulting the Army Selection Table provided for the Pitched Battle Scenario (scenario 1, section 2).

(5) *Defender Suffers Attrition.* The Defender rolls a die and removes the number of units indicated (to account for the usual confusion of warfare).

Die Roll	Units Lost
1–2	3
3–4	2
5–6	1

(6) *Attacker Selects Flanking Force.* The Attacking general selects his or her army by rolling a die and consulting the Army Selection Table for the Pitched Battle Scenario (scenario 1, section 2).

(7) *Attacker Suffers Attrition.* The Flanking Force rolls a die and removes the number of units indicated (accounting for the tendency of units to take the wrong turning in any march around an enemy flank).

Die Roll	Units Lost
1–2	3
3–4	2
5–6	1

(8) *Defender Deploys Army.* The Defending general sets up his or her army within 15cm of the Southern baseline. No unit may deploy within 15cm of the Western or Eastern table edges.

(9) *Begin the Game.* The Attacker takes the first turn. The Flanking Force appears anywhere on the Western table edge on Turn 1.

SCENARIO 5: THE MINIGAME

Many wargamers have grandiose ambitions, wanting as they do to play massive games with hundreds of figures on tables of 240cm × 150cm (8′ × 5′) or even larger. These projects are very seductive, but fail to take account of the fact that not everyone has access to such huge areas. This is why my games are all postulated around the arena of a 120cm × 90cm (4′ × 3′) table, which should be within the logistical reach of most households. However, there comes a time when an even smaller game is required, which is where the minigame comes in. This is essentially a Pitched Battle fought with five units on each side over an area of 60cm × 60cm (2′ × 2′). It may not have the scope of its larger counterparts, but allows for very quick games fought over a convenient small area – in addition to

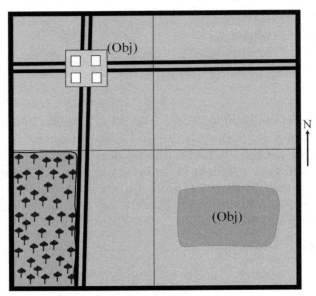

Map 2. A Suggested Battlefield: Scenario 5

diminutive armies requiring a minimum of time to paint. Mini-games can even be taken on holiday, for those who wish to pursue their wargaming in a different environment.

(1) *How to Win.* Both objectives must be controlled by the end of Game Turn 10.

(2) *Army Selection.* Each wargamer rolls a die and consults the table below, in order to ascertain the constituent units of his or her army.

Unit Type

Die Roll	Infantry	Skirmishers	Cavalry	Artillery
1	2	1	1	1
2	3	1	1	0
3	3	0	1	1
4	3	0	2	0
5	3	0	0	2
6	3	1	0	1

(3) *Determining Sides.* Both players roll a die, with the winner deciding on whether he or she wishes to Attack or Defend.

(4) *Deployment Area.* The Defender rolls a die to determine which table edge will form his or her baseline.

Die Roll	Table Edge
1–2	North
3–4	South
5	West
6	East

(5) *Pre-Battle Events.* These are the same as the Pitched Battle Scenario, with the exception that fewer units are affected by each event. As with the Pitched Battle, both sides roll a die and act according to the appropriate result:

Die Roll	Event
1–2	Bogged Down
3–4	Traffic Congestion
5–6	Flank March (Attacker)
	Forward Deployment (Defender)

(a) *Bogged Down*. One unit (which must be Artillery if applicable) is eliminated.

(b) *Traffic Congestion*. Two units (at least one of which must be Infantry) arrive late. Roll a die to determine the turn on which they appear on the friendly baseline:

Die Roll	Turn
1–2	2
3–4	3
5–6	4

(c) *Flank March*. Two Attacking units (at least one of which must be Cavalry if available, and none of which may be Artillery) appear on either enemy flank. The Attacking general chooses which at the start of the game, and rolls a die to determine the turn on which the flanking force arrives:

Die Roll	Turn
1–2	2
3–4	3
5–6	4

(d) *Forward Deployment*. Two Defending units set up within 30cm of their baseline. Artillery may not be selected.

(6) *Defender Deploys Army*. The Defender sets up his or her army within 15cm of its baseline (or 30cm for any units eligible for Forward Deployment).

(7) *Attacker Deploys Army*. The Attacking army is set up within 15cm of its baseline (apart from units engaging on a Flank March).

(8) *Begin the Game*. The Attacker always goes first in every Game Turn.

Chapter 5

Wargames Army Lists

The lists provided below are intended to fight the scenarios featured in the previous chapter. Readers will soon become aware that some armies are decidedly more capable than their historical antagonists – a situation that will doubtless appal those wargamers who demand contrived equality in their contests, but which should be welcomed by those who prefer a degree of realism.

The lists are designed to invoke the character of each individual army, and also the specific theatres of war in which they operated. These goals are realised through the medium of giving each army a selection of special rules, so that any wargamer feels that he or she is commanding a force that is grounded in its time and place, rather than an amorphous and rather anonymous generalised entity with little specific flavour.

VARIABLE NUMBERS

Many special rules provide for the reclassification of a variable number of units. For example, the army list for Radetzky's Austrian Army allows 1–3 Infantry units to be upgraded from Average to Elite morale. To generate the precise number required, roll a die and refer to the table printed below:

Numerical Spread

Die Roll	0–1	1–2	1–3	1–6
1	0	1	1	1
2	0	1	1	2
3	0	1	2	3
4	1	2	2	4
5	1	2	3	5
6	1	2	3	6

Variable Numbers in Minigames

The numbers listed in the special rules refer to the standard sized scenarios. For minigames (and also the defending side in the Rearguard Action scenario), the relevant spread of variable numbers can be found by consulting the table below:

Numbers in Standard Scenarios	Numbers in Minigames
1–6	1–3
1–3	1–2
1–2	0–1
0–1	0

Optional Leadership Rules

Chapter 2 referred to the prevailing wargames fashion for including detailed rules for command and control, and to my decidedly unfashionable lack of enthusiasm for them. It would however be churlish to ignore the leadership dimension altogether, especially as the nineteenth-century battlefield did raise real difficulties over the command and control of armies. This was mainly due to the problems arising as forces grew increasingly larger, as indeed did the area over which they fought.

It should be stressed that these rules are optional, and should only be adopted if both players agree to their use. They work on the assumption that a variable number of units are 'In Command' in each turn; these may move and fire without any restrictions. Skirmishers are always in command, due to their inherent ability to act independently. So far as other units are concerned, the player rolls a die at the start of his or her turn to find out how many units are in command. He or she should consult the table below for the result, which is dependent upon the Command Level given in each army list:

Command Level

Die Roll	Poor	Average	Good
1–2	2	4	6
3–4	3	5	7
5–6	4	6	8

These numbers apply for standard scenarios; they are always halved in minigames (and for defenders in the Rearguard Action scenarios). Fractions should always be rounded up.

Units that are 'Out of Command' may only move at half their normal speed and may only roll half their normal allocation of dice when firing during their own turn (again, fractions should always be rounded up). These rules are designed to reflect a situation whereby the army commander is prioritising the operations of some units and ignoring others: the neglected unfortunates lack both direction (hence their restricted movement) and supply priority (which accounts for why they need to conserve their ammunition).

Wargamers should note that defensive fire against enemy charges is never penalised; for this was a genuinely critical situation and firepower would accordingly be maximised without reference to supply constraints.

ARMY LISTS

The army lists take up the remainder of this chapter. Readers are strongly advised to only fight encounters between armies which either engaged each other historically, or could have done so potentially. There is nothing to stop wargamers attempting to have a contest between (for example) the Italian Army of 1848 and the Prussian Army of 1870, but such encounters would be remarkably pointless, quite apart from being exceptionally one-sided in favour of the Prussians.

It should be noted that some of the special rules listed below are optional, and as such should only be adopted if both players agree to their use.

Revolutionary Army (1815–1848)
Unit Types
> Regular Infantry (Average, Smoothbore Musket, Close Order)
> National Guard Infantry (Levy, Smoothbore Musket, Close Order)
> Mob Infantry (Rabble, Smoothbore Musket, Close Order)
> Skirmishers (Elite, Smoothbore Musket)
> Artillery (Smoothbore)

Special Rules
(1) *Infantry Composition.* 1–3 units are National Guard, the remainder are Regular (for Mobs, see below).

(2) *Mob Infantry*. This army does not field any Cavalry units. They are replaced by Mob Infantry units. Mob Infantry may only operate in Column formation.

(3) *Insurgents*. 1–2 of these units may be placed anywhere on the battlefield, after both armies have deployed. They are classified as Skirmishers (Rabble, Smoothbore Musket).

(4) *Command Level* (Optional). This army is rated as Poor.

Commentary

This rather generic army is designed to depict a typical revolutionary force that featured in the various attempts to overthrow the old order. Its enthusiasm invariably exceeded its competence, which explains the low morale rating of many troops (reflecting lack of discipline) and poor leadership (reflecting the lack of trained officers). I have however assumed that some Regular units could have joined the Revolutionaries, especially from the ranks of the Skirmishers and Artillery: these tended to attract more educated and less socially-exclusive officers, many of whom were sympathetic to liberalism and nationalism. The same could not be said of the Cavalry, whose aristocratic ethos invariably transferred into loyalty to the old order.

The Mob and Insurgent units are included to convey an impression of an armed citizenry. These were completely untrained, unlike the National Guard militia, and were therefore of minimal fighting value. The Mobs tended to huddle together in a columnar formation, whereas the Insurgents are assumed to lurk with evil intent in wooded or urban areas, operating as Skirmishers and sniping at the enemy.

Monarchical Army (1815–1848)

Unit Types

Infantry (Average, Smoothbore Musket, Close Order)
Skirmishers (Elite, Smoothbore Musket)
Cavalry (Average)
Artillery (Smoothbore)

Special Rules

(1) *Reactionary Fervour*. 1–3 units are upgraded by one morale level. Cavalry units must always be reclassified first.

(2) *Command Level* (Optional). The army is rated as Average.

Commentary

The armies of the old régimes were always superior to their rather motley bunch of Revolutionary enemies; as Chapter 1 pointed out, the monarchies kept their armies small and disciplined, precisely in order to ensure social exclusivity (with the necessary exception of those technical branches requiring an educated officer corps) and consequent political reliability.

The special rule covering 'Reactionary Fervour' depicts the great enthusiasm some units had for suppressing any revolution, preferably with extreme brutality. Such traits were especially pronounced amongst the Cavalry, whose officers were always drawn from the most aristocratic and conservative elements of the state.

Spanish Carlist Army (First Carlist War: 1833–1837)
Unit Types
Infantry (Elite, Smoothbore Musket, Loose Order)
Skirmishers (Fanatic, Smoothbore Musket)
Cavalry (Average)
Artillery (Smoothbore)

Special Rules
(1) *Fanaticism.* 1–3 Infantry units are upgraded to Fanatic morale.
(2) *Limited Cavalry.* 1–2 Cavalry units are replaced by Skirmishers.
(3) *Limited Artillery.* 1–2 Artillery units are replaced by Skirmishers.
(4) *Command Level* (Optional). This army is rated as Good.
(5) *Limited Numbers* (Optional). Only 0–1 Artillery units may be fielded; any remaining Artillery units are removed from the army and not replaced (if this rule is used, the special rule covering Limited Artillery no longer applies).
(6) *Rugged Terrain* (Optional). Charging units have their move restricted to 8cm.

Commentary

The Carlist army was noted for its numerical inferiority, the fanaticism of its soldiers, and the quality of its leadership. Unfortunately for the Spanish reactionaries, their military superiority was never enough to offset their political unpopularity on the national level.

The Carlists frequently operated in rugged terrain, where Skirmishers proved to be of greater utility than either Cavalry or

Artillery, which explains why the latter two arms fielded few units. There were other reasons why few horsemen and guns were fielded, however. The Cavalry was never able to secure a decent supply of quality horses, and also suffered from having the majority of the regular army's mounted troops serve with the Cristino forces; the Artillery could seldom secure much ordnance.

The optional rule covering rugged terrain may not appear especially swingeing, but appearances are deceptive: the rule serves to reduce the effectiveness of Cavalry by allowing the smoothbore musket an extra move of shooting prior to being charged. This will force any wargamer to take great care when using his or her mounted units.

Spanish Cristino Army (First Carlist War: 1833–1837)
Unit Types
Cristino Infantry (Average, Smoothbore Musket, Loose Order)
British Auxiliary Legion Infantry (Average, Smoothbore Musket, Close Order)
British Royal Marines Infantry (Fanatic, Smoothbore Musket, Close Order)
Skirmishers (Average, Smoothbore Musket)
Cavalry (Average)
Artillery (Smoothbore)

Special Rules
(1) *Infantry Composition.* The wargamer may choose to field units of the British Auxiliary Legion. If he or she does so, then 1–2 Infantry units are classified as British Auxiliary Legion; 0–1 units are British Royal Marines; and the remainder are Cristino Infantry.
(2) *Cristino Unreliability.* 1–6 Cristino Infantry or Cavalry units are downgraded to Levy morale. The wargamer may choose which units are affected.
(3) *Limited Cavalry.* 0–1 Cavalry units are replaced by Skirmishers.
(4) *Limited Artillery.* 0–1 Artillery units are replaced by Skirmishers.
(5) *British Riflemen.* 0–1 Skirmisher units may be replaced by the Rifle contingent of the British Auxiliary Legion (classified as Skirmishers, with Elite morale and smoothbore muskets).

(6) *Command Level* (Optional). This army is rated as Average.

(7) *Rugged Terrain* (Optional). Charging units have their move restricted to 8cm.

Commentary

This list covers the Legitimist Cristino Army of the First Carlist War. The Spanish Legitimist cause had the happy ability to attract the support of those who favoured the established order, and also the many liberals who were appalled at the ideologically reactionary nature of the Carlists (whose refusal to countenance female succession of the Spanish throne served to prompt the Carlist Wars). This political strength was just as well, for the Cristino army was never more than mediocre: its strength lay chiefly in its numerical superiority, especially where Cavalry and Artillery units were concerned. However, the rugged terrain of the battlefields rendered Skirmishers especially useful, and these troops were to play a vital role in both the Carlist and Cristino armies.

The British Auxiliary Legion was a body of volunteers recruited to serve the Cristino cause. Further details of this body of men can be found in Chapter 8. It should however be noted that the British never mastered the art of operating in loose order, which would have proved extremely useful in the rugged Spanish terrain; their Infantry units do as a consequence have to fight in close order formation.

Radetzky's Austrian Army (Italian Revolt: 1848–1849)

Unit Types

Infantry (Average, Smoothbore Musket, Close Order)
Skirmishers (Average, Smoothbore Musket)
Cavalry (Elite)
Artillery (Smoothbore)

Special Rules

(1) *Veteran Infantry*. 1–3 Infantry units are upgraded to Elite morale.

(2) *Command Level* (Optional). This army is rated as Good.

(3) *Broken Terrain* (Optional). This has the following effects:

  (a) Charging units have their move reduced to 8cm.

  (b) Units in open terrain have a saving roll of 5–6 if shot at.

Commentary

The octogenarian Field Marshal Radetzky may have been elderly, but was also exceptionally efficient; he was able to turn his army into a quality instrument of war, which routed its Italian opponents with little difficulty.

Radetzky's army has been classified to reflect its attributes, and not simply in its command status. The Field Marshal inspired a great deal of affection, which is why some Infantry units enjoy an upgrade to Elite status – a level already attained by the Hapsburg Cavalry, which had always enjoyed a high reputation. The Skirmishers have been downgraded to Average morale however; this reflects the extent to which these had been influenced by revolutionary ideas – some units had a distinctly lukewarm allegiance to the Hapsburg cause.

The Italian landscape was covered with irrigation ditches, trees, and hamlets. These do not seem to have impeded normal movement, but did disrupt charges: these required an expanse of flat terrain if they were to acquire full impetus, especially for Cavalry. As a consequence, the movement rate for charging units has been reduced to 8cm in a deliberate attempt to reduce the effectiveness of horsemen. The assorted elements of broken terrain also affected fire owing to the cover they provided.

Italian Army (Italian Revolt: 1848–1849)

Unit Types
> Piedmontese Infantry (Average, Smoothbore Musket, Close Order)
> Italian Infantry (Levy, Smoothbore Musket, Close Order)
> Bersaglieri Skirmishers (Fanatic, Smoothbore Musket)
> Piedmontese Cavalry (Average)
> Italian Cavalry (Levy)
> Artillery (Smoothbore)

Special Rules
(1) *Infantry Composition.* 1–3 Infantry units are Italian; the remainder are Piedmontese.
(2) *Cavalry Composition.* 0–1 Cavalry units are Italian; the remainder are Piedmontese.
(3) *Command Level* (Optional). This army is rated as Poor.

(4) *Broken Terrain* (Optional). This has the following effects:
   (a) Charging units have their move restricted to 8cm.
   (b) Units in open terrain have a saving roll of 5–6 if shot at.

Commentary

The Italian army of 1848 was far from being a united national entity, which had serious effects upon its military performance. Many of the minor states had little attachment to nationalism and even less to liberalism: they only entered the war owing to popular pressure. There was also much doubt as to the desirability of swapping one regional power (the Hapsburg Empire) in favour of the dominance of another (the Kingdom of Piedmont). Many troops therefore had questionable morale; only the Piedmontese had any reliability – especially the élite Bersaglieri Skirmishers. The generally unfortunate situation was compounded by distinctly indifferent leadership. It was therefore scarcely surprising that the Italian Army was no match for Radetzky's Austrians.

Danish Army (First Schleswig War: 1848–1850)
Unit Types
   Infantry (Average, Smoothbore Musket, Close Order)
   Skirmishers (Elite, Smoothbore Musket)
   Cavalry (Average)
   Artillery (Smoothbore)

Special Rules
(1) *Rifled Muskets.* 1–2 units are equipped with these weapons. They must be assigned to Skirmishers; any remaining rifles may then be allocated to Infantry units.
(2) *Naval Transport.* The army receives the services of an additional 1–2 Infantry units.
(3) *Command Level* (Optional). This army is rated as Average.
(4) *Espignols.* These extremely primitive multi-barrelled weapons were attached to Artillery units. Accordingly, Artillery may roll an additional die when firing at short range (up to 12cm). This additional die is treated as if it were an Infantry unit in Column formation.
(5) *Broken Terrain* (Optional). This has the following effects:
   (a) Cavalry movement is restricted to 12cm.

(b) Charging units have their move restricted to 8cm.

(c) Units in Open Terrain have a saving roll of 5–6 if shot at by Infantry or Skirmishers.

Comentary

The Danish Army of the First Schleswig War was a thoroughly competent force, whose efficiency can chiefly be explained by the fact that most of its officers stayed loyal. The contribution of the Danish Navy was especially important, allowing as it did for additional units to arrive by sea. The army also had some access to rifled muskets.

The Danish landscape featured irrigation canals and earthen banks; the latter provided a degree of cover, and served to impede movement, particularly of mounted units. As for the Espignols, these exceptionally primitive early attempts at machine gun technology do not seem to have had much effect: the rule is included as an option for those wargamers who wish to add a touch of period flavour.

Schleswig-Holstein Army (First Schleswig War: 1848–1850)
Unit Types
Schleswig-Holstein Infantry (Levy, Smoothbore Musket, Close Order)

Prussian Infantry (Average, Smoothbore Musket, Close Order)

Skirmishers (Average, Smoothbore Musket)

Cavalry (Levy)

Artillery (Smoothbore)

Special Rules
(1) *Infantry Composition.* 1–2 Infantry units are Prussian; the remainder are Schleswig-Holstein Infantry.

(2) *Rifled Muskets.* 1–6 units are equipped with these weapons. They must first be allocated to Skirmishers; remaining allocations may equip Schleswig-Holstein Infantry units.

(3) *Dreyse Needle Guns.* 0–1 Prussian Infantry units are equipped with Early Breechloading Rifles.

(4) *Command Level* (Optional). This army is rated as Poor.

(5) *Espignols* (Optional). These extremely primitive multi-barrelled weapons were attached to Artillery units. Accordingly, Artillery may roll an additional die when firing at short range (up to 12cm). This additional die is treated as if it were an Infantry unit in Column formation.

(6) *Broken Terrain* (Optional). This has the following effects:

(a) Cavalry movement is restricted to 12cm.

(b) Charging units have their move restricted to 8cm.

(c) Units in open terrain have a saving roll of 5–6 if shot at by Infantry or Skirmishers.

Commentary

The Schleswig-Holstein Army was nowhere near as effective as its Danish opponent, due primarily to its constant failure to recruit officers of the requisite quality. This had a serious effect upon the morale and performance of the units. The rebels did however enjoy access to the Danish Army arsenal, which they captured early in the war; they secured a ready supply of Pillar Breech Rifles as a result (these are rated as Rifled Muskets in the rules).

The Schleswig-Holstein Army did enjoy some assistance from the Prussians, whose presence can be explained by the revolutionary ferment sweeping the German territories in 1848. These sentiments were emphatically not shared by the Prussian monarchy, but the latter felt compelled to send some units to help the ethnic Germans in Schleswig-Holstein. Some of the Prussian Infantry were equipped with the new Dreyse Needle Guns; these can add an intriguing dimension to any wargame.

British Army (Crimean War: 1854–1856)

Unit Types

Infantry (Elite, Rifled Musket, Close Order)
Skirmishers (Fanatic, Rifled Musket)
Cavalry (Elite)
Artillery (Smoothbore)

Special Rules

(1) *Infantry Drill.* Infantry units may move in Line formation.

(2) *Command Level* (Optional). This army is rated as Average.

Commentary

The British Army of the Crimean War has had a rather bad press over the following century and a half, chiefly due to its occasionally idiosyncratic higher command. It is certainly true that strategic leadership was not of the highest order; but command on a tactical level was usually competent, and the troops themselves superbly disciplined. Their morale was exceptionally high, and the Infantry's combination of training and *esprit de corps* even enabled them to move in Line formation.

Russian Army (Crimean War: 1854–1856)
Unit Types
   Infantry (Average, Smoothbore Musket, Close Order)
   Cavalry (Average)
   Artillery (Smoothbore)

Special Rules
(1) *No Skirmishers*. This army does not field any Skirmisher units. Any mandated Skirmishers are replaced by Artillery units.
(2) *Cossacks*. 1–2 units of Cossacks (Dragoons, Rabble, Smoothbore Musket) are added to this army (in addition to all its other units).
(3) *Columnar Tactics*. Infantry units may only operate in Column formation.
(4) *Stubborn Infantry*. The first time a base is removed from Infantry units after enemy shooting, Russian Infantry automatically pass the ensuing morale test.
(5) *Command Level* (Optional). This army is rated as Poor.
(6) *Charge of the Light Brigade* (Optional). The Russian player rolls a die at the start of each British turn. On the first occasion he or she rolls a 6, the Russian wargamer may command a single British Cavalry unit for the duration of that turn. This event may only occur once during the wargame.

Commentary
The Russian Army was in a bad state during the Crimean War, suffering as it did from poor training and appalling leadership. The former is accounted for by the special rules covering 'No Skirmishers' and 'Columnar Tactics'; the latter by the low command rating.
   The Russians did however have some advantages. They were invariably supplied with an extremely generous provision of

Artillery units, and also had the services of the legendary (if seldom especially efficient) Cossacks.

I suspect that most wargamers will want some provision for covering the 'Charge of the Light Brigade', which is why the relevant optional rule has been included. Conflating singular events in this manner does not represent good wargaming design practice, but will certainly provide a good deal of suitably eccentric period flavour. The Russians should enter into the spirit of the occasion by sending the unfortunate British Cavalry unit towards the nearest enemy Artillery concentration!

French Army (Franco-Austrian War: 1859)
Unit Types
Line Infantry (Average, Rifled Musket, Loose Order)
Chasseurs Infantry (Elite, Rifled Musket, Loose Order)
Skirmishers (Elite, Rifled Musket)
French Cavalry (Average)
Piedmontese Cavalry (Elite)
Artillery (Smoothbore)

Special Rules
(1) *Infantry Composition.* 1–2 Infantry units are Chasseurs; the remainder are Regular Infantry.
(2) *Cavalry Composition.* 0–1 units are Piedmontese Cavalry; the remainder are French.
(3) *Infantry Elan.* Infantry units may always charge their enemy counterparts, even if they have fewer bases than the latter.
(4) *Rifled Artillery.* 0–1 units have Bronze Rifled guns.
(5) *Command Level* (Optional). This army is rated as Average.
(6) *Broken Terrain* (Optional). This has the effect of giving units in open terrain a saving roll of 5–6 when shot at.

Commentary
The French Army of 1859 was not especially well led, but was noted for its aggressive Infantry tactics, which proved spectacularly successful against rifled muskets, especially given the extra cover provided by the broken terrain that was such a feature of Italy. It should be noted that this terrain no longer provided such a serious obstacle to the movement of units operating in loose order.

The Piedmontese Cavalry units provided vital assistance to the French, frequently performing exceptionally well: this is why they merit Elite classification.

Austrian Army (Franco-Austrian War: 1859)
Unit Types
Infantry (Average, Rifled Musket, Loose Order)
Austrian Skirmishers (Elite, Rifled Musket)
Croat Skirmishers (Levy, Rifled Musket)
Cavalry (Average)
Artillery (Smoothbore)

Special Rules
(1) *Skirmisher Composition.* 0–1 units are Austrian; the remainder are Croats.
(2) *Command Level* (Optional). This army is rated as Poor.
(3) *Broken Terrain* (Optional). This has the effect of giving units in open terrain a saving roll of 5–6 when shot at.

Commentary
The Austrian Army of 1859 was in a very poor state, with leadership at an especially low ebb (things would have turned out much better had the recently deceased Field Marshal Radetzky still been alive). All units underperformed as a result, with the Croat skirmishers putting in a particularly bad display, owing to their increasing disaffection with Hapsburg imperial rule.

The standard of Austrian Infantry musketry was notably feeble, largely owing to lack of firearms practice on the grounds of cost cutting. I have not chosen to penalise Infantry capability however, assuming that the lack of training was largely offset by the acknowledged superiority of the Austrian Lorenz Rifle to most of its European counterparts in other armies.

Garibaldini Army (War of Italian Liberation: 1860)
Unit Types
Infantry (Fanatic, Smoothbore Musket, Loose Order)
Skirmishers (Fanatic, Smoothbore Musket)
Artillery (Smoothbore)

Special Rules
(1) *No Cavalry.* This army does not have any Cavalry units. They are not replaced by other units.
(2) *Limited Artillery.* This army may only field one Artillery unit. Any additional Artillery units may not be replaced by other troop types.
(3) *Assault Doctrine.* The following rules apply to Infantry units:
    (a) they must remain in Column formation throughout the game.
    (b) they may charge Neapolitan Cavalry units.
    (c) they may always declare a charge, even if they have fewer bases than their target unit.
(4) *Command Level* (Optional). This army is rated as Good.

Commentary
Garibaldi's Army consisted largely of fanatical idealists who made up in determination for what they lacked in numbers and equipment. The lack of modern weaponry was due largely to the fact that their Piedmontese sponsors distrusted them; Guiseppe Garibaldi's extreme liberalism was decidedly alien to the constitutional monarchy of Piedmont.

Neapolitan Army (War of Italian Liberation: 1860)
Unit Types
    Infantry (Rabble, Rifled Musket, Loose Order)
    Skirmishers (Rabble, Rifled Musket)
    Cavalry (Rabble)
    Artillery (Smoothbore)

Special Rules
(1) *Terror.* All units must take a morale test when Garibaldini Infantry declare a charge upon them.
(2) *Timorous Infantry.* Neapolitan Infantry may never charge Garibaldini units.
(3) *Feeble Cavalry.* Neapolitan Cavalry only roll 2 dice per base if charging, and 1 die per base if defending.
(4) *Command Level* (Optional). This army is rated as Poor.

Commentary
The Neapolitan Army had a terrible reputation under its Bourbon monarchy. Despite having reasonable equipment, the levels of corruption and incompetence were such that the troops were appallingly trained by their venal officer corps. As a result, all units were prone to running away at the earliest possible opportunity. They were certainly no match for their Garibaldini opponents.

Danish Army (Second Schleswig War: 1864)
Unit Types
　　Infantry (Levy, Rifled Musket, Loose Order)
　　Skirmishers (Average, Rifled Musket)
　　Cavalry (Levy)
　　Artillery (Bronze Rifled)

Special Rules
(1) *Enhanced Morale.* 1–6 units of the player's choice may be upgraded one level.
(2) *Danes and Prussians.* The following rules apply when Danish Infantry are fighting the Prussian Army:
　　(a) they must remain in Column formation until reduced to 2 bases.
　　(b) they may always charge Prussian Infantry, provided that the Danish unit has at least 3 bases – even if the Prussian unit is of equal or superior strength.
(3) *Command Level* (Optional). This army is rated as Average.
(4) *Broken Terrain* (Optional). The following rules apply for units in open terrain:
　　(a) Cavalry movement is restricted to 12cm.
　　(b) Infantry and Artillery movement is restricted to 8cm.
　　(c) units that charge have their movement restricted to 8cm.
　　(d) units shot at by Infantry or Skirmishers have a saving roll of 5–6.

Commentary
The Danish Army was all too conscious that it faced overwhelming odds in the Second Schleswig War, opposed as it was by both Austria and Prussia. The Danes had moreover just reorganised their troops, which disrupted the army at a spectacularly inopportune

moment. Their army has a fairly low base morale level as a result, although its reasonable performance in the field allows for some units to be upgraded.

The Danish Infantry had a defensive posture when facing the rather aggressive Austrian tactics, but did espouse assault doctrine when fighting the more passive Prussians. The Danes soon became aware of the power of the Prussian rifles however; as a consequence, their predilection for bayonet charges tended to be of limited duration: this is why units with 2 bases remaining may revert to Line formation.

The broken terrain that played a part in the First Schleswig War still featured in 1864. The irrigation canals and earth banks both impeded movement and provided cover.

Prussian Army (Second Schleswig War: 1864)
Unit Types
Infantry (Average, Early Breechloading Rifle, Loose Order)
Skirmishers (Elite, Early Breechloading Rifle)
Cavalry (Average)
Artillery (Smoothbore)

Special Rules
(1) *Dubious Morale.* 1–6 units of the player's choice are downgraded one morale class.
(2) *Krupp on Trial.* 0–1 Artillery units are Steel Rifled.
(3) *Command Level* (Optional). The Prussian player rolls a die at the start of the game. The command level is Poor on a roll of 1–2; Average on a roll of 3–4; and Good on a roll of 5–6.
(4) *Broken Terrain* (Optional). The following rules apply for units in open terrain:
(a) Cavalry movement is restricted to 12cm.
(b) Infantry and Artillery movement is restricted to 8cm.
(c) units that Charge have their movement restricted to 8cm.
(d) units shot at by Infantry or Skirmishers receive a saving roll of 5–6.

Commentary
The Prussian army of 1864 was a long way from being all-conquering. General von Moltke's reforms were only beginning to take

effect, and many units suffered rather indifferent morale during the interim. Command performance was similarly variable: both morale and competence have been accounted for in the special rules listed above.

The Krupp steel artillery was only beginning to equip the Prussian Army at this point; its potential was only to be fully realised in 1870, which is why its usage before then is restricted.

Austrian Army (Second Schleswig War: 1864; Seven Weeks War: 1866)

Unit Types
Infantry (Average, Rifled Musket, Loose Order)
Skirmishers (Elite, Rifled Musket)
Cavalry (Elite)
Artillery (Bronze Rifled)

Special Rules
(1) *Bayonets of the Empire*. The following rules apply to Austrian Infantry units:
  (a) they must remain in Column formation.
  (b) they may always charge enemy Infantry units, irrespective of relative strength levels.
(2) *Lorenz Rifle*. Austrian Infantry units always roll one additional die when firing.
(3) *Command Level* (Optional). The following levels apply to the Austrian Army:
  (a) 1864. The army is rated as Good.
  (b) 1866 (Germany). The army is rated as Average.
  (c) 1866 (Italy). The army is rated as Good.
(4) *Aggressive Artillery* (Optional). If the Command rules are used, a single Artillery unit is activated automatically, without expending any Command Points.
(5) *Broken Terrain* (Optional). The following rules apply for units in open terrain in the Danish campaign of 1864:
  (a) Cavalry movement is restricted to 12cm.
  (b) Infantry and Artillery movement is restricted to 8cm.
  (c) Units shot at by Infantry and Skirmishers receive a saving roll of 5–6.

(6) *Tree-Lined Battlefield* (Optional). Units fighting in Italy in 1866 enjoy a saving roll of 5–6 from enemy fire.

Commentary

The Austrians had learned the lessons of their 1859 experience, where inertia had handed the initiative to their French enemies. The consequent development of an aggressive Infantry and Artillery doctrine, relying upon bayonet assaults in the case of the former and the exercise of initiative with the latter arm (equipped with new bronze rifled guns), was to prove very effective against most armies. Unfortunately for the Hapsburgs, they failed to realise that the Prussian Infantry's breechloading rifles had changed the agenda: the Austrian assault doctrine was perfectly equipped for fighting the war of 1864; it was not so well adapted for the Prussians in 1866.

The variable Command Levels of this army are explained by its generals. General Gablenz (the commander in 1864) and Archduke Albert (the leader in Italy in 1866) were exceptionally capable commanders; General Benedek (the commander in Germany in 1866) was not at the same level – some harsh critics might consider that the Austrian Army of 1866 only deserves a poor classification when fighting in Germany. I suspect this is rather too severe (and also makes the assault doctrine exceptionally difficult to carry out); Benedek's army may however be classified as having a Poor command status if the wargamer is feeling uncharitable.

Moltke's Prussian Army (Seven Weeks War: 1866)
Unit Types
Infantry (Elite, Early Breechloading Rifle, Loose Order)
Skirmishers (Fanatic, Early Breechloading Rifle)
Cavalry (Average)
Dragoons (Average, Early Breechloading Rifle)
Artillery (Smoothbore)

Special Rules
(1) *Cavalry Composition.* 0–1 units are Dragoons; the remainder are Cavalry.
(2) *Krupp on Trial.* 0–1 Artillery units are Steel Rifled.
(3) *Command Level* (Optional). This army is rated as Good.

Commentary

The principal Prussian Army of 1866 was a formidable instrument of war, proving more than a match for its Austrian opponents. This was due to a combination of the infantry with its Dreyse Needle Gun, and the highly capable leadership displayed at every level.

The only weakness of the Prussian Army lay in its Artillery, whose equipment and doctrine was still at an early stage of development. The special rule allowing for the limited presence of Dragoons reflects the training of the latter units; it could however be argued that all Prussian mounted troops operated in a shock role, a decision which can be taken at the discretion of the wargamer.

Prussian Army of The Main (Seven Weeks War: 1866)
Unit Types
Regular Infantry (Average, Early Breechloading Rifle, Loose Order)
Landwehr Infantry (Levy, Rifled Musket, Loose Order)
Skirmishers (Elite, Early Breechloading Rifle)
Cavalry (Average)
Dragoons (Average, Early Breechloading Rifle)
Artillery (Smoothbore)

Special Rules
(1) *Infantry Composition*. 1–3 units are Landwehr; the remainder are Regular.
(2) *Enhanced Morale*. 1–3 units are upgraded one morale level. The Prussian player may choose which units to upgrade, with the exception that Landwehr Infantry may never be reclassified.
(3) *Krupp on Trial*. 0–1 Artillery units are Steel Rifled.
(4) *Cavalry Composition*. 0–1 units are Dragoons; the remainder are Cavalry.
(5) *Command Level* (Optional). This army is rated as Average.

Commentary
One of General Moltke's greatest qualities as a commander was his sense of priorities. He realised that the best Prussian troops had to face the Austrian Army, whereas Austria's allies in western Germany could be dealt with by lower quality soldiers and lesser commanders. This is why the Army of the Main has a contingent of

Landwehr reserve troops, and why much of the rest are not up to the standard of the forces under Moltke's command. All this does provide for some extremely interesting battles – wargamers should never forget that commanding a lesser army can be a far more exacting challenge than leading an all-conquering force.

Hanoverian Army (Seven Weeks War: 1866)
Unit Types
  Infantry (Average, Rifled Musket, Loose Order)
  Skirmishers (Elite, Rifled Musket)
  Cavalry (Average)
  Artillery (Smoothbore)

Special Rules
(1) *Enhanced Morale.* 1–6 units of the player's choice are upgraded one morale level.
(2) *Command Level* (Optional). This army is rated as Good.

Commentary
The Hanoverian Army was by far the most formidable of the Army of the Main's opponents. Its chief difficulties were strategic: it lacked abundant supplies of ammunition, and could not mobilise rapidly enough to move southwards and join with its allies. In the wargaming context however, the Hanoverians are likely to put up a very good fight against the Army of the Main: the better troops and more capable leadership of the former have to confront the breechloading rifles of the latter.

Bavarian Army (Seven Weeks War: 1866)
Unit Types
  Infantry (Levy, Rifled Musket, Loose Order)
  Skirmishers (Average, Rifled Musket)
  Cavalry (Levy)
  Artillery (Smoothbore)

Special Rules
(1) *Veterans.* 1–6 units of the player's choice are upgraded one morale level.
(2) *Krupp on Trial.* 1–2 Artillery units are reclassified as Steel Rifled.
(3) *Command Level* (Optional). This army is rated as Poor.

Commentary

The Bavarian Army was the largest of the Army of the Main's opponents in 1866, fighting several engagements against the latter force. Bavarian morale suffered owing to equivocal motivation (the troops were disinclined to fight other Germans over what was perceived as a purely dynastic struggle) and some decidedly poor leadership. The troops did however become quite experienced very quickly; the better units rose to the challenge with sufficient alacrity to merit the provisions of the 'Veterans' special rule.

The Bavarians were supplied with some Krupp steel guns, just like the Prussians. They seem to have realised the potential of these weapons rather more quickly than the Army of the Main: they may accordingly upgrade 1–2 Artillery units rather than the 0–1 allocated to the Prussians.

Federal German Army (Seven Weeks War: 1866)

Unit Types

German Infantry (Average, Rifled Musket, Loose Order)
Baden Infantry (Levy, Rifled Musket, Loose Order)
Skirmishers (Elite, Rifled Musket)
Cavalry (Average)
Artillery (Smoothbore)

Special Rules

(1) *Infantry Composition.* 1–2 units are Baden Infantry; the remainder are German.
(2) *Assault Doctrine.* 1–2 German Infantry units are affected by this rule, for which the following stipulations apply:
  (a) the units must remain in Column formation throughout the game.
  (b) the units may always charge enemy Infantry units, irrespective of relative strength levels.
(3) *Krupp on Trial.* 1–2 Artillery units are reclassified as Steel Rifled.
(4) *Command Level* (Optional). This army is rated as Poor.

Commentary

The Federal German Army (it was nominally only a Corps sized formation) was the last of the Army of the Main's opponents in 1866. It was a distinctly heterogeneous entity, being composed of

1. The Polish Insurrection (1831). Polish rebels await their Russian foes from behind a barricade. (Photograph by Richard Ellis Photography/*Miniature Wargames* magazine)

2. 'Steady Boys!' The mounted Polish general encourages his men to stand firm. (Photograph by Richard Ellis Photography/*Miniature Wargames* magazine)

3. The First Carlist War (1833–1837). The Carlist forces attack a village held by their Cristino enemies. (Photograph by Richard Ellis Photography/*Miniature Wargames* magazine)

4. 'To the bayonet!' The Cristino infantry charges its foe. (Photograph by Richard Ellis Photography/ *Miniature Wargames* magazine)

5. The Battle of Miloslaw (1848). The Poles fight for their freedom again, this time against a Prussian force. 25mm figures by Dorset Soldiers. (The Continental Wars Society)

6. The Polish patriots assault the Prussian lines. 25mm figures by Dorset Soldiers. (The Continental Wars Society)

7. Radetzky's march. The Austrian army launches a concerted assault upon the Italians at the Battle of Novara (1849). 42mm figures by Shiny Toy Soldiers. (The Continental Wars Society)

8. The somewhat demoralised Italians await the Austrian onslaught at Novara. 42mm figures by Shiny Toy Soldiers. (The Continental Wars Society)

9. The Charge of the Light Brigade. The remnant of the British 17th Lancers approaches the Russian guns at the Battle of Balaclava (1854). Figures painted by Kevin Dallimore. (Kevin Dallimore)

10. The Crimean War (1854–1856). French forces defend a river against a Russian assault.
(Photograph by Richard Ellis Photography/*Miniature Wargames* magazine)

11. The crisis point of the battle is reached, with the French preparing to repel the Russian attack.
(Photograph by Richard Ellis Photography/*Miniature Wargames* magazine)

12. Wargame conventions allow for the display of massive wargames. This game uses 15mm figures to depict the French and Austrian armies clashing at the Battle of Solferino (1859). It was presented by the Newbury and Reading Wargames Society. (Photograph by The Continental Wars Society)

13. Another view of the Solferino wargame. (Photograph by The Continental Wars Society)

14. This group of Prussian infantry wears the feldmutz field cap, rather than the more famous pickelhaube helmet. 25mm figures by Helion. (North Star Military Figures Ltd)

15. A unit of Prussian uhlans on patrol. 25mm figures by Helion. (North Star Military Figures Ltd)

16. The wrong way to do it. This Austrian storm column from the Seven Weeks War is about to be destroyed by Prussian firepower. 25mm figures by Helion. (North Star Military Figures Ltd)

17. The right way to try it. These Austrian infantrymen have formed a firing line. 25mm figures by Helion. (North Star Military Figures Ltd)

18. The Austrian cavalry was the pride of the 1866 army. This is a unit of hussars. 25mm figures by Helion. (North Star Military Figures Ltd)

19. The Krupp rifled artillery proved decisive during the Franco-Prussian War (1870–1871). This Bavarian example was painted by Kevin Dallimore. (Kevin Dallimore)

20. This Franco-Prussian clash shows the Prussian cavalry about to dispose of its French counterparts. (Photograph by Richard Ellis Photography/*Miniature Wargames* magazine)

21. The Prussian infantry assaults the French village. (Photograph by Richard Ellis Photography/ *Miniature Wargames* magazine)

22. 6mm figures allow for wargames to be fought on very small tables. This French army is designed to be used with my rules. 6mm figures by Baccus. (Baccus 6mm Ltd)

23. A Prussian 6mm army configured for my rules. Figures by Baccus. (Baccus 6mm Ltd)

24. The Battle of Gravelotte–St Privat (1870). The right wing of the Prussian Guard Corps is about to be shattered when attacking St Privat. 6mm figures by Baccus. (Baccus 6mm Ltd)

25. The Prussian Guard Corps' central component launches a diversionary attack. 6mm figures by Baccus. (Baccus 6mm Ltd)

26. The decisive blow. The success of the left wing of the Prussian Guards led to the capture of Roncourt – and the subsequent outflanking of the French line. 6mm figures by Baccus. (Baccus 6mm Ltd)

27. The French defenders of Roncourt await their fate. 6mm figures by Baccus. (Baccus 6mm Ltd)

28. The Battle of Loigny–Poupry (1870). The French advance on Loigny. 6mm figures by Baccus. (Baccus 6mm Ltd)

29. The French clash with Bavarian troops outside Loigny. Note how flags can aid unit recognition with diminutive miniatures. 6mm figures by Baccus. (Baccus 6mm Ltd)

30. The French centre at Loigny–Poupry encounters the Prussian advance guard outside the village of Lumeau. 6mm figures by Baccus. (Baccus 6mm Ltd)

31. The Prussian main body deploys behind Lumeau, ready to reinforce the advance guard. 6mm figures by Baccus. (Baccus 6mm Ltd)

32. A Prussian division deploys from marching column into a firing line. 6mm figures by Baccus. (Baccus 6mm Ltd)

33. This French infantry unit has every intention of relying on the firepower of its Chassepot rifles. 6mm figures by Baccus. (Baccus 6mm Ltd)

elements from Baden, Württemburg, Hesse-Darmstadt, Nassau, and Austria. Most of the troops fought well, despite the somewhat eccentric leadership provided by Prince Alexander of Hesse. The only exception was the Baden contingent, whose loyalties were divided between Austria and Prussia.

As might be expected with such a polyglot army, tactical doctrine varied between its elements. This was especially notable amongst the Infantry contingents, some of which espoused the assault doctrine preferred by the Austrians, whilst others adopted the Prussian reliance upon musketry.

Italian Army (Seven Weeks War: 1866)
Unit Types
Infantry (Levy, Rifled Musket, Loose Order)
Bersaglieri Skirmishers (Fanatic, Rifled Musket)
Cavalry (Average)
Artillery (Bronze Rifled)

Special Rules
(1) *Command Level* (Optional). This army is rated as Poor.
(2) *Tree-Lined Battlefield* (Optional). Units in open Terrain enjoy a saving roll of 5–6 from enemy firing.

Commentary
The Kingdom of Italy had delusions of grandeur following its unification, and was convinced that its Army could defeat the Austrians. The catastrophic 1866 campaign, which saw the Italians routed at the Battle of Custoza, showed that such beliefs were hopelessly optimistic. The chief problem lay in the difficulties of incorporating central and southern Italy into a state dominated by the erstwhile Kingdom of Piedmont; many elements believed that they were simply exchanging the rule of one empire (the Hapsburgs) for another (the Piedmontese). All this had serious military ramifications, with many elements of the new Italian Army lacking motivation – this was especially true of the Infantry. The one exception to this rather gloomy picture was provided by the Bersaglieri units, who continued to show the exceptionally high motivation for which they were renowned.

The special rule for Tree-Lined Battlefields refers to conditions applying at Custoza, where observation was so limited as to have a detrimental effect upon both small arms and artillery fire.

French Imperial Army (Franco-Prussian War: 1870)
Unit Types

Regular Infantry (Average, Later Breechloading Rifle, Loose Order)

Imperial Guard or Zouave Infantry (Elite, Later Breechloading Rifle, Loose Order)

Skirmishers (Fanatic, Later Breechloading Rifle)

Cavalry (Average)

Artillery (Smoothbore)

Special Rules
(1) *Infantry Composition.* 1–2 units are Imperial Guard or Zouaves; the remainder are Regular.
(2) *Rifled Artillery.* 0–1 Artillery units are reclassified as Bronze Rifled.
(3) *Mitrailleuse.* Artillery units roll one extra die when firing at short range (up to 12cm).
(4) *Command Level* (Optional). This army is rated as Poor.
(5) *Infantry Support* (Optional). The Mitrailleuse special rule no longer applies. Instead, 1–2 Infantry units of the player's choice may re-roll any dice registering a miss when shooting.

Commentary
The French Imperial Army of the Franco-Prussian War was a potentially fine instrument of war. It was however ruined by execrably poor leadership. Wargamers can take comfort from the excellence of the Chassepot infantry rifle, and deplore the inferiority of the Artillery. The latter was in reality equipped with bronze rifled pieces, but these suffered both from inferior doctrine (they were invariably held back in reserve, never committing to the decisive point of the battlefield) and from defective ordnance (the fuses of the shells often malfunctioned, which resulted in many failing to explode).

The French expected a great deal from the Mitrailleuse. This early machine gun was a potentially decisive weapon, but it suffered from being deployed with the Artillery, rather than with the Infantry. The optional rule covering Infantry Support is included for those players who wish to explore what might have been.

French Republican Army (Franco-Prussian War: 1870–1871)
Unit Types
Regular Infantry (Average, Later Breechloading Rifle, Loose Order)

Foreign Legion or Zouave Infantry (Elite, Later Breechloading Rifle, Loose Order)

Garde Mobile Infantry (Levy, Rifled Musket, Loose Order)

Skirmishers (Fanatic, Later Breechloading Rifle)

Cavalry (Average)

Artillery (Bronze Rifled)

Special Rules
(1) *Infantry Composition.* 1–3 units are Garde Mobile; 0–1 are Foreign Legion or Zouave; the remainder are Regular.

(2) *Francs-Tireurs.* 1–2 units of these irregular volunteer troops are positioned anywhere on the table, immediately after both armies have deployed. They are classified as Skirmishers (Rabble, Smoothbore Musket).

(3) *Command Level* (Optional). This army is rated as Average.

(4) *Garibaldini* (Optional). The wargamer rolls a die before the Francs-Tireurs units deploy. On a roll of '6', a single unit may be reclassified as Garibaldini Skirmishers (Fanatic, Smoothbore Musket).

Commentary
Following the defeat of Napoleon III in September 1870, the new French Republican government carried on the struggle. A quasi-popular army was promptly recruited (much to the horror of the Prussians, who considered such developments as falling outside the bounds of civilised warfare). It did moreover perform rather better than its Imperial predecessors, despite the poor equipment and uncertain morale of Garde Mobile and Francs-Tireurs units. This higher level of performance was due primarily to superior leader-ship: this is expressed not only in the Command Level, but also in

the Artillery classification; the Bronze Rifled ordnance was finally deployed more aggressively, and performed better as a result.

The optional rule for Garibaldini covers the presence of Guiseppe Garibaldi himself, who fought for the new Republican government along with a contingent of his followers. This remarkable man's revolutionary ardour had not diminished with the passing of time, and he was still willing to fight for democratic values even into his sixties.

Prussian Army (Franco-Prussian War: 1870–1871)
Unit Types
Infantry (Elite, Early Breechloading Rifle, Loose Order)
Skirmishers (Fanatic, Early Breechloading Rifle)
Cavalry (Average)
Dragoons (Average, Early Breechloading Rifle)
Artillery (Steel Rifled)

Special Rules
(1) *Cavalry Composition.* 0–1 units are Dragoons; the remainder are Cavalry.
(2) *Command Level* (Optional). This army is rated as Good.
(3) *Von Bredow* (Optional). 0–1 Cavalry units may be reclassified as Fanatic.
(4) *Bavarian Infantry* (Optional). 1–2 Prussian Infantry units are replaced by Bavarian Infantry (Average, Rifled Musket, Loose Order).

Commentary
The Prussian Army was a truly formidable instrument of war by 1870, and its quality leadership ensured that its troops outclassed their French opponents. The wargames table will see a fascinating clash between the superior French Chassepot infantry rifles, and the Prussian Krupp steel guns.

The optional rule for von Bredow's Cavalry covers the slim possibility of replicating that commander's stunning success at the battle of Mars-La-Tour (see Chapter 14). As for the Bavarian Infantry, they played a significant role in many engagements during the Franco-Prussian War – wargames generals should resist the temptation to exclude them simply because of their inferiority!

Russian Army (Russo-Turkish War: 1877)
Unit Types
Infantry (Average, Early Breechloading Rifle, Loose Order)
Dragoons (Average, Early Breechloading Rifle)
Artillery (Bronze Rifled)

Special Rules
(1) *Bayonets of the Empire.* Infantry units must remain in Column formation for the duration of the game. They may however always charge enemy Infantry units, irrespective of relative strength levels.
(2) *No Skirmishers.* This army does not field any Skirmisher units; they are replaced with additional Artillery units.
(3) *Stubborn Infantry.* The first time a base is removed from Infantry units after enemy shooting, Russian Infantry automatically pass the ensuing morale test.
(4) *New Rifles.* 1–2 Infantry units are equipped with Later breechloading Rifles.
(5) *Cavalry Classification.* All Cavalry units are classified as Dragoons.
(6) *Command Level* (Optional). The Russian player rolls a die at the start of the game. On a roll of 1–2 the command level is Poor; on a 3–6 it is Good.

Commentary
This army is an interesting mixture of rather dated Infantry assault doctrine, and an exceptionally modern approach to mounted warfare. The Russians were the only European army to learn the lessons of the American Civil War, and expected their cavalry to fight dismounted in the manner of that conflict.

Russian leadership was rather variable. Generals Skoboleff and Gourko were capable commanders; the same could not unfortunately be said of other leaders.

Ottoman Army (Russo-Turkish War: 1877)
Unit Types
Regular Infantry (Elite, Later Breechloading Rifle, Loose Order)
Militia Infantry (Levy, Early Breechloading Rifle, Loose Order)
Bashi-Bazouk Skirmishers (Rabble, Smoothbore Musket)

Dragoons (Levy, Rifled Musket)
Artillery (Steel Rifled)

Special Rules

(1) *Infantry Composition.* 1–2 units are Militia; the remainder are Regular.

(2) *Entrenchments.* Infantry units may deploy in entrenchments. They are treated as being in a Wood.

(3) *Cavalry Composition.* All Cavalry units are classified as Dragoons.

(4) *Command Level* (Optional). The Ottoman player rolls a die at the start of the game. On a roll of 1–4 the army is rated as Poor; on a roll of 5–6 it is rated as Average.

Commentary

The problem of grafting a European-style organisation onto a basically tribal host, was not a new one for the Ottoman Empire. The result was a collection of decidedly variable troops: the Regular Infantry were for example second to none; whereas the semi-criminal gangs of Bashi-Bazouks were second to all. The Regular Infantry and Artillery were however extremely well-equipped, and provide an interesting challenge for the Russian Army.

Ottoman leadership was frequently dreadful. Some commanders, especially Osman Pasha (the defender of the fortress of Plevna) did however rise to the challenge, which is why this force can occasionally achieve Average command status.

Chapter 6

Wargaming Historical Battles

Many wargamers see the simulation of historical battles as the summit of their art, given that this involves both the direct re-enactment of an historical situation, and for salutary reflection upon momentous events through the medium of a wargame. Its mechanics are moreover straightforward enough: the players need to find a good account of a decisive engagement, construct the necessary terrain, and field the correct numbers of troops according to the selected scale. This will allow the wargamers to appreciate the full scope of the nineteenth-century battlefield.

There are however some significant difficulties with the approach outlined above. The first of these concerns the size of the battles in question – they could be fought by well over 100,000 men on each side, over an area of several miles. Such engagements can only be simulated through a massive team effort: many wargamers will have to be enlisted to paint the thousands of figures required, and a large venue will have to be hired for the occasion. The use of diminutive 6mm figures makes such enterprises more practical, but will still involve a tremendous amount of work. Accordingly, the representation of historical battles to particular scales is only possible if tiny, indecisive engagements are to be simulated. These are often extremely enjoyable occasions, but the senses of occasion and significance will inevitably be lost.

It could of course be argued that mere difficulties should never deter the wargamer from pursuing his or her goal. Fighting a great historical battle in miniature with thousands of figures is the sort of event one can take part in with great pride – and remember with pleasure for the rest of one's life. Those wargamers who specialise in such massive enterprises will always deserve and receive the respect of the entire hobby. Nevertheless, there are serious difficulties resulting from the very concept of true scales, which have already been considered in Chapter 2. As a result, there is little point in attempting to achieve a literal representation or re-creation that cannot possibly be realised. The only escape from this dilemma is either to adopt the 'free *kriegspiel*' or gridded tables approach discussed previously, or instead to radically alter the scale. The latter involves using one base of figures to represent thousands of men, and to have a single centimetre depict at least a hundred metres. This approach was pioneered by C.F. Wesencraft in two chapters of his masterwork *Practical Wargaming*, and also considered by the late Paddy Griffith in his similarly magnificent *Napoleonic Wargaming For Fun*. Such wargames are certainly viable, but their focus is inevitably directed towards command and control rather than tactical interaction. As a result, the visual appeal of distinct units of painted figures equipped with particular weaponry is lost – and a good deal of the value of miniature wargaming with it.

There is however much more to the hobby than the direct re-creation of historical battles. For the apparently secondary goal of allowing the wargamer to reflect upon historical events is in reality the key to any successful game. An appreciation of this acts as a liberation: true historical understanding can be engendered by using a wargame to create the correct atmosphere – and not simply a slavish reproduction to a rigid scale. If the look and feel of an historical engagement can be replicated on the wargames table, then the dilemmas which beset the original commanders can be reproduced; and players will then be in a position to form a true appreciation of historical events.

The key to simulating any historical battle lies in replicating the tactical situation that afflicted the original generals. This no longer requires an exact re-creation of a battlefield to scale; an average sized wargames table can now suffice, so long as the most significant terrain pieces from the original engagement can be placed upon it. Similarly, the relative proportions of the armies can be reproduced, rather than absolute downscaling. One can for example consider a battle where one army was 100,000 strong, whereas its rival had 80,000 men. If this is reproduced to an absolute scale of a single figure representing 50 men, then 2,000 figures will face 1,600. However, if the relative proportions of 5:4 are adopted, then the larger force could number for example 100 figures, whereas its rival would comprise 80 miniatures. This is far more manageable, and can reflect the true situation just as effectively. I have adopted the latter approach; I do however use the principle of unit rather than figure ratios, so that the relative proportions of opposing units give a correct impression of what happened historically.

The series of chapters which follow are devoted to simulating historical battles. They start with an historical account to establish the context. There follows a description of the wargames forces involved, along with a map setting out their deployment, and a separate statement of reinforcement schedules (if applicable). Any special rules affecting the conduct of the game are then outlined if appropriate. In some cases, optional rules are included to examine plausible events that could have affected the outcome of the battle, if they had occurred on the day of the real engagement. These were referred to as 'Military Possibilities' by Donald Featherstone in his classic work devoted to re-creating historical battles, *Battle Notes for Wargamers*. They can provide an intriguing glimpse into alternative decisions or events that could have altered history – a possibility that will appeal to all wargamers, and which has often proved a strong motivating force in re-creating historical battles in the first place.

THE MAPS
The maps provided with each chapter are intended to help players set up wargames at home. Each square represents an area of 30cm × 30cm, which should be very suitable for most games; however, in cases where the unit base widths are unusually narrow or exceptionally wide, the size of the table should be altered in proportion.

Chapter 7

The Battle of Alegria (27 October 1834)

HISTORICAL ACCOUNT

The First Carlist War began in 1833 with a dispute over the succession to the Spanish throne (not for the first or indeed the last time in history). The argument arose between reactionaries, who believed that the Spanish monarch should always be a male, and liberals (a decidedly relative term in the Spanish context) who were not so hidebound.

For as long as King Ferdinand VII remained childless, this presented no problem; his brother Carlos would succeed him. All this changed when Ferdinand married Maria Cristina of Naples, and was persuaded by his new wife to set aside the Salic Law, which had been in force since 1713 and which only permitted succession through the male line. The consequent fury of conservatives was exacerbated when Maria Cristina gave birth to a daughter, Isabella, in 1830. The king's subsequent untimely death in 1833 led to a civil war between the conservatives who supported Don Carlos' claim to the throne (and who became known as Carlists), and the liberal partisans of the Regent Maria Cristina ruling on behalf of her infant daughter (these liberals were referred to as Cristinos).

The Carlists were strongest in northern Spain, and their brighter leaders soon realised that their best approach lay in achieving local superiority over the Cristinos. This was only possible in the north, for the Spanish regular army was controlled by the Cristinos, and proved itself fully capable of exerting control over central and southern Spain. The Carlists were however highly motivated, frequently being of superior fighting quality to their opponents. As a consequence, they often won battles, and were moreover capable of launching expeditions into Cristino territory. These latter forays were however of limited utility, since the Carlists never had enough

92

men to hold the areas they captured, since the mobility that was the expeditions' greatest asset necessitated the commitment of small forces. The Cristinos were ultimately to win the war simply by holding onto the territory they already controlled, and by waiting for the political divisions within the Carlist camp to take a hold.

The Battle of Alegria, fought on 27 October 1834, was a fairly typical engagement of the early stage of the First Carlist War, seeing as it did an ambush of a small Cristino army by a larger Carlist force. In this case, 4,700 Carlists under General Zumalacárregui detected a 3,200 strong Cristino army under General O'Doyle (who like many Spanish generals was of Irish descent) at Alegria, near Vitoria.

Zumalacárregui was a particularly gifted general, and hit upon a plan which made the most of his forces. He hoped to entice an attack by splitting his forces, leaving a portion of his army facing the Cristinos, allowing O'Doyle to believe that he enjoyed overall numerical superiority. Meanwhile, General de Iturralde would lead the rest of the Carlist army in an attack upon the right flank of the Cristinos.

O'Doyle promptly obliged by attacking the Carlist main army, doubtless hoping that his two artillery pieces would have a decisive effect upon an enemy army which lacked any ordnance. Unfortunately for O'Doyle, the Cristino army suffered from very low morale at this early stage of the war – only a few units of the old regular army could be relied upon, with many newly raised contingents being very suspect. As a consequence, the Cristino assault soon bogged down when it became obvious that its immediate target, the élite Carlist Guias de Navarre unit, proved itself ready, willing and decidedly able to stand its ground. A firefight broke out as a result. The appearance of Iturralde's flanking contingent was however to turn the stalemate into a decisive Carlist victory, with the cavalry of the latter proving to have a great appetite for slaughtering the vanquished foe. O'Doyle's army promptly disintegrated and, in a process that was to prove a depressingly familiar event of the war, many prisoners were shot, including the vanquished General O'Doyle.

THE WARGAME
Game Duration
The game lasts a total of 8 turns. The Cristino player goes first in each turn.

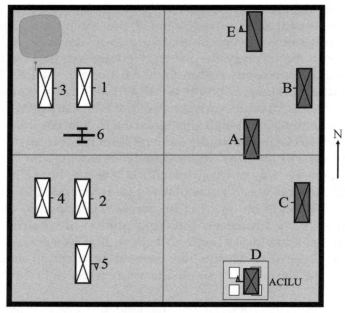

Map 3. The Battle of Alegria

Wargame Forces: The Cristino Army
O'Doyle's army is deployed on the table at the start of the game, as illustrated on the map. Its foremost units are deployed 15cm from the western edge of the table.

Unit Type	Map Designation
Infantry (Average, Smoothbore Musket, Loose Order)	1
Infantry (Levy, Smoothbore Musket, Loose Order)	2, 3
Infantry (Rabble, Smoothbore Musket, Loose Order)	4
Skirmishers (Average, Smoothbore Musket)	5
Artillery (Smoothbore)	6

The Cristino army did not perform well at Alegria, which is why only one of the Infantry units receives an Average morale level. This is assumed to be a better trained or more highly motivated unit of the Regular army. Those units rated as levies are assumed to be unenthusiastic Regulars, whereas the unit classed as Rabble represents a hastily raised and barely trained contingent. The Skirmishers are included to account for their presence at most battles of the war;

they have been deployed away from the Carlist Cavalry to allow for basic tactical insights (no commander would ever have positioned Light Infantry in close proximity to enemy horsemen, as this would almost guarantee the annihilation of the former with some rapidity).

Wargame Forces: The Carlist Army

Zumalacárregui's army is divided into two groupings. The main force is deployed on the table as shown on the map, with the foremost units arrayed 15cm from the eastern table edge.

Unit Type	Map Designation
Guias de Navarre Infantry (Fanatic, Smoothbore Musket, Loose Order)	A
Infantry (Elite, Smoothbore Musket, Loose Order)	B, C
Skirmishers (Fanatic, Smoothbore Musket)	D
Cavalry (Average)	E

I worked on the basis that the Carlist Infantry enjoyed excellent morale, having as they did an exceptionally high motivation for their cause, and being led by a remarkably able general. The Guias de Navarre had the greatest reputation of all the army, and have been classified as Fanatics as a result. I felt it appropriate to include a unit of Skirmishers, in keeping with their prominence during the war – these too have been granted enhanced morale in keeping with the independent spirit invariably displayed by such troops. The Cavalry does not enjoy such a high status; Spain did not have much of a tradition of mounted warfare, largely owing to the inhospitable nature of much of the terrain. This, combined with the extreme difficulty the Carlists had in raising a cavalry contingent from scratch, results in their being allocated Average morale status.

So far as deployment is concerned, I placed the Guias de Navarre to the fore, in keeping with their role during the battle. The units of Skirmishers and Cavalry present greater problems, however. The former have been allocated to the village of Acilu, allowing them to provide unfettered fire support for the army, as well as a measure of protection to its left flank. This allows the Cavalry, which was historically divided into two small contingents with one on each flank, to be fielded as one complete unit on the right – it would otherwise have had to be fielded as two half sized units, which would have diminished its impact to an unacceptable degree.

Iturralde's flanking force consists of the following:

Unit Type	Unit Designation
Infantry (Elite, Smoothbore Musket, Loose Order)	F, G
Skirmishers (Fanatic, Smoothbore Musket)	H

These troops enter the game as reinforcements. Their arrival is determined by having the Carlist player roll a die at the start of each Carlist movement phase from Turn 2 onwards. The flanking force appears as soon as the Carlist player achieves a score of 5–6. It arrives anywhere along the southern edge of the table.

Special Rules
There are no Special Rules for this battle scenario.

Optional Military Possibilities
(1) *Carlist Confusion*. Flanking marches always had the possibility of degenerating into chaos as units lost their way. To account for this, Iturralde's flanking force only appears if the Carlist player achieves a die roll of 6 (rather than 5–6) when testing to see if Iturralde arrives.
(2) *Cristino Morale*. It is possible that O'Doyle's army was in an even more shaky state than I have rated them. This can be accounted for by reclassifying Infantry unit 1 as Levy, and Infantry unit 3 as Rabble.

Victory Conditions
(1) *Carlist Victory*. The Carlists must destroy all Infantry units of the Cristino army in order to win the game.
(2) *Cristino Victory*. The Cristinos must exit two Infantry units from the Eastern edge of the table in order to achieve victory. The game ends the instant the second unit leaves the table.
(3) *Draw*. If neither side achieves its victory conditions, the result is a Draw.

Chapter 8

The Battle of Oriamendi (16 March 1837)

HISTORICAL ACCOUNT

One of the most notable features of the First Carlist War was the presence of a large British contingent on the Cristino side. This force was created thanks to the initiative of the Spanish Ambassador to London, General Miguel de Alava (a noted Anglophile who had served on Wellington's staff during the Napoleonic Wars). Alava hoped to win British support for the liberal Cristino cause, and found a staunch ally in the person of Viscount Palmerston, the Whig Foreign Secretary. The latter was able to persuade King William IV to authorise the enlistment of a British Auxiliary Legion, recruited and paid for under the auspices of the Spanish government.

The fact that the Legion was part of the Spanish army was of great legal importance; it meant that Britain herself played no official part in the First Carlist War, whilst allowing her nevertheless to provide tangible support to the Cristino cause. A force of 10,000 men was recruited very quickly, although it must be said that this rapid enlistment created its own problems. Chief among these lay in the field of leadership, whose difficulties stemmed from a political impasse. For the British Tory Party was distinctly unwilling to sponsor any involvement in foreign military adventures – some Tories were so thoroughly conservative that they had a good deal of sympathy for the reactionary Carlists. One especially noted opponent of foreign intervention in Spanish affairs was the Duke of Wellington, who refused to allow serving regular British army officers to enlist in the Legion. As a result, the latter was forced to recruit former officers of liberal sympathies, who were willing to risk losing their rather ungenerous pension in order to serve in the Legion. These recruitment difficulties led to many officers serving in higher ranks than they had previously attained. The example of the Legion's commander, George de Lacy Evans, is an especially apposite one. Evans had served with distinction in the Napoleonic Wars, ending it as a Colonel. By 1835 his notably liberal views had led to his membership of the Radical Party, and successful election as MP for Westminster. However, for all his undoubted merits Evans had to make the rapid leap from the retired Colonel of 1818 to the serving General of 1835. This resulted in a decidedly steep learning curve – an experience which was all too common for the Legion's officers, and which inevitably had an effect upon the new army's performance.

Recruitment of an officer corps may have proved problematic; the same was not true where the other ranks were concerned. For the post-Napoleonic period saw appalling rural poverty: enclosure had already seen the end of smallholdings, with their previous tenants forced to work as labourers for the very landowners who had seized their acreage; and the rise of industrialisation was rendering the old textile skills obsolete. The ensuing hardship saw much political agitation for increased voting rights, which bore only limited fruit with the Reform Act of 1832. It also gave rise to rioting in the countryside, with farming machinery a particular target. It was therefore not surprising that many men seized the opportunity of enlistment in the British Auxiliary Legion, if only as a means of avoiding the brutish squalor that was their everyday lot. This was especially true of Ireland, the poverty of whose inhabitants was frequently exacerbated by religious tensions: their Roman Catholicism met with vehement opposition from the Protestantism usually espoused by the large landowners.

By 1836 the Legion had arrived in Spain, and proved itself to be a competent force, albeit not of the standard of the British regular army. In particular, its officers never succeeded in the art of rapid manoeuvre over the difficult Spanish terrain – the British Auxiliary Legion invariably operated in close order, as opposed to the looser formation adopted by the indigenous Carlist and Cristino armies.

The start of 1837 saw the Cristino forces ready to take the offensive, following the Carlist failure to capture Bilbao. A rather complicated plan was devised, whereby three separate Cristino armies were to converge upon and destroy the Carlist forces. Such arrangements often look good on paper, but executing them invariably proves rather more difficult. They rely upon rapid movement and efficient co-ordination on the part of the attacker, combined with an obliging inactivity from their prospective victim. Unfortunately for the Cristinos, both ingredients were lacking. Two of the attacking columns, under General Baldomero Espartero and Pedro Sarsfield (an officer who was, like the unfortunate General O'Doyle we met in the previous chapter, of Irish descent) achieved nothing owing to their timid leadership. The British Auxiliary Legion formed the bulk of the third column, and General de Lacy Evans proved himself to be a decidedly more effective commander than his timorous colleagues. His column erupted from its base at San Sebastian, and on 15 March 1837 managed to drive the Carlists off the eminence of Oriamendi Hill. The following day saw Evans preparing to mop up the remaining Carlist forces, which were defending the town of Hernani.

Unfortunately for the British general, the Carlists' overall commander, Don Sebastian de Borbon, was a man of great resource and initiative, both of which traits now came to the fore. De Borbon had noted that the dilatory attacks from Espartero and Sarsfield were unlikely to achieve anything; he accordingly disengaged all the units facing those two worthies, promptly uniting his entire command to confront the far more dangerous Evans. Both antagonists numbered around 10,000 men; unfortunately for the British Auxiliary Legion, Evans had no idea that he was about to be attacked. The consequent surprise was to prove unanticipated, unwelcome and exceptionally unpleasant.

De Borbon's army was divided into three parts, and proceeded to assault the British right, centre and left in a remarkably co-ordinated manner – especially given the rapidity with which the Carlists were forced to consolidate their host. Evans' army was sent reeling by de Borbon's assault and panic ensued. The attack on the British left flank was especially effective, led as it was by the 6th Guipuzcoa Battalion. This unit had a penchant for shock tactics, and the prospect of receiving cold steel proved too much for its foes, who promptly ran away. This victory in turn facilitated the success of the Carlist assault upon the Cristino centre, which saw de Borbon's men capture Oriamendi Hill.

Fortunately for Evans, his right wing stood firm, thanks largely to staunch resistance both from his Legion, and also from a battalion of

Royal Marines. As a part of Britain's regular armed forces, the latter should not legally have been present with the Legion. However, they had provided assistance in the original disembarkation of the British volunteers, and had contrived to stay on – the British government turning a convenient blind eye to such unorthodox activity. The Marines were nevertheless ordered not to play too active a role in any fighting; but they were fully prepared to help succour Evans' retreat, which did not thereby become a rout.

The Carlist victory at Oriamendi was still tactically significant, although the strategic consequences were to prove baleful for the pretender to the Spanish throne. For the Carlists promptly became overconfident, embarking upon a large scale foray into Cristino territory. The Royal Expedition, as it became known, ranged far and wide: it did however lack both the numerical and political strength necessary to prevail; its sole effect was to prove that Carlism was a mere regional entity, with no power base outside northern Spain. As a consequence, Don Carlos' cause was doomed to fail.

THE WARGAME
Game Duration
The game lasts a total of 15 turns. The Carlist player goes first in each turn.

Wargame Forces: The Carlist Army
Most of de Borbon's army is deployed on the table at the start of the game, as illustrated on the map provided.

Unit Type	Map Designation
Infantry (Elite, Smoothbore Musket, Loose Order)	1, 2, 4, 6, 7, 9, 11, 12
6th Guipuzcoa Infantry (Fanatic, Smoothbore Musket, Loose Order)	10
Cavalry (Average)	5
Artillery (Smoothbore)	3, 8

The Carlist army can also draw upon the services of 3 units of Skirmishers (Fanatic, Smoothbore Musket). These deploy within 12cm of any Carlist Infantry unit.

De Borbon's army was an exceptionally highly motivated force, which is why all foot units have been given such formidable morale

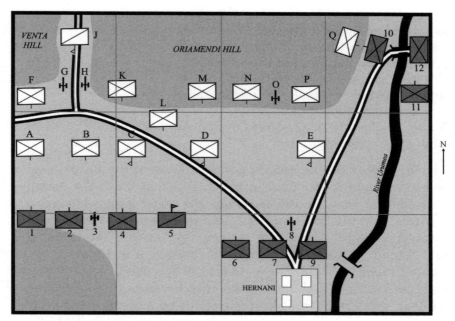

Map 4. The Battle of Oriamendi

ratings. The impact (in every sense) of the 6th Guipuzcoa Infantry is reflected not only in its high morale, but also in the special rule listed below. Its tendency to charge any enemy unit regardless of casualties must be depicted; one can argue that Oriamendi would never have been won without such reckless bravery.

It will be noted that the Cavalry lacks such benefits. This is because the Carlist horse never seems to have performed especially well, as discussed in the previous chapter. The undulating terrain at Oriamendi certainly had an effect upon its impetus, as reflected in the special rule listed below.

Wargame Forces: The Cristino Army

General de Lacy Evans' army is deployed on the table at the start of the game. Its positions are indicated on the map provided.

Unit Type	Map Designation
Cristino Infantry (Average, Smoothbore Musket, Loose Order)	**A, B, M, P**

Cristino Skirmishers (Average, Smoothbore Musket)	**C, D, E**
Royal Marines Infantry (Fanatic, Smoothbore Musket, Close Order)	**F**
British Auxiliary Legion Infantry (Average, Smoothbore Musket, Close Order)	**K, L, Q**
British Auxiliary Legion Rifles Infantry (Elite, Smoothbore Musket, Close Order)	**N**
British Auxiliary Legion Lancers Cavalry (Average)	**J**
Artillery (Smoothbore)	**G, H, O**

I have worked on the assumption that most of the British Legion was competent rather than inspired, and that the Rifles battalion was slightly more motivated than the other units. I have also assumed that the latter unit operated in close order rather than its Napoleonic skirmishing role (principally because the designated unit actually represents a combined contingent of Riflemen and a standard legionary battalion). As for the Spanish Cristino Infantry, their performance had improved somewhat from the early years of the war, meriting Average morale status as a result. Readers who disagree can use the optional downgrading provided in the Military Possibilities.

Special Rules

(1) *The Mighty 6th.* The awesome achievements of the Carlist 6th Guipuzcoa Infantry are depicted by allowing the unit to charge any enemy unit at any time, irrespective of relative base strengths.

(2) *Cristino Confusion.* The Carlist assault engendered extreme panic in the Cristino army. All units of Evans' army must test morale at the start of each of the first 3 Carlist turns.

(3) *Cavalry Limitations.* The unpromising terrain of the battlefield seems to have restricted the activities of horsemen. Cavalry charge moves are therefore reduced to 8cm.

(4) *Unfordable River.* The river Urumea may only be crossed via the two bridges indicated on the map.

(5) *High Politics.* As discussed earlier, the activities of the Royal Marines were circumscribed by political restrictions. Accordingly, the Royal Marines may not move further than 8cm from the Venta Hill.

Military Possibilities

(1) *Uncoordinated attack.* De Borbon's improvised attack could easily have been afflicted by confusion. To account for this possibility, the Carlist player rolls a die at the start of the game. The indicated number of units (which must be Infantry or Cavalry) do not appear until the start of Turn 4.

(2) *Prepared Defence.* General Evans was somewhat remiss in failing to even consider the possibility of a Carlist counter attack on 16 March. If the wargamer would like to consider what might have happened with better preparation, apply the following rules:

(a) The special rule for Cristino Confusion no longer applies.

(b) 1–6 Infantry units of the Cristino army (roll a die to decide how many) begin the game entrenched. For rules purposes, this is the equivalent of occupying a town.

(3) *Cristino Morale.* Those who are convinced of the continued ineptitude of Spanish Cristino forces may downgrade all Spanish Cristino Infantry to Levy morale.

(4) *British Alliance.* To account for the highly unlikely prospect of a formal British alliance, apply the following rules:

(a) The Royal Marines no longer have any movement restrictions; they are assumed to play a full and active role in Evans' army.

(b) An additional British Auxiliary Legion unit of the Cristino player's choice is upgraded to Elite morale status. This reflects a political decision to allow British regular army officers to join the Legion.

Victory Conditions

Whichever army has the greatest number of units occupying Oriamendi Hill at the end of the game is the winner. If the number of units is equal, then the Cristino player is assumed to have narrowly repelled the Carlist assault, and to have achieved a marginal victory.

Chapter 9

The Battle of The Alma
(20 September 1854)

HISTORICAL ACCOUNT

Students of history are doubtless aware of the rather depressing tendency of religious tensions to result in political and military conflict. This phenomenon was all too apparent in the case of the Crimean War, which saw its origins in a dispute over the jurisdiction of Christian Holy Places in what is now Israel. These were controlled by the Ottoman Empire in the nineteenth century; and tensions arose when the Turks allowed Catholic Christians greater rights over the administration of the relevant locations. This aroused the ire of the Orthodox Church, which had hitherto enjoyed exclusive rights over the jurisdiction of Christian Holy Places. As a result, a conflict between Catholic and Orthodox establishments ensued – and with the former supported by France, and the latter enjoying Russian patronage, the theological dispute soon acquired a political dimension.

The religious issue may have provided an excuse for conflict; there was rather more to the Crimean War than a rather petty confrontation over ecclesiastical administration. The real issue lay over Russian ambitions with respect to Ottoman territory: she was especially intent upon seizing control of the Black Sea and the Dardanelles Straits. If these ends could be attained, then Russia would enjoy ready access to the Mediterranean Sea, thereby allowing both for increased trade and the projection of Russian naval power; the Tsar would moreover effectively control the politically decrepit Ottoman Empire as a result.

Britain and France were exceptionally worried about the Russian bear flexing its muscles, and vowed to assist the Turkish Sultan in his hour of need. The intensification of tension led to both western powers declaring war upon Russia in March 1854.

The first allied objective was to block the Russian assault upon Ottoman territory. However, the Turks themselves showed that they were not entirely bereft of military ability, and had halted the Tsar's armies in what is now Bulgaria. By the time the western forces arrived on the scene, they found that the Ottomans no longer needed liberating: the war's objectives had been achieved. The most logical step would have been for the British and French forces to return home. This would not however have accounted for public opinion, which in Britain especially was spoiling for a fight – secure in the knowledge that as civilians, they would not be called upon to risk their own lives. As a result of this pressure, a new objective was agreed upon. It was felt that the Anglo-French seizure of the Crimean Peninsular was desirable, since this would result in the control of the Russian naval base of Sebastapol, which would render the Tsar's maritime ambitions null and void.

The Crimea was duly invaded on 14 September, as an expeditionary force comprising 30,000 French, 27,000 British, and 5,000 Ottoman troops landed. A rather disorderly advance towards Sebastapol ensued. Deficiencies in army leadership and administration became all too apparent – with no conflict having been fought between the major European powers since 1815, all sides were badly out of practice, and were woefully unprepared for the rigours of campaigning. However, on 20 September the first battle of the Crimean offensive occurred when the western allies encountered the Russian army at the River Alma.

The Tsarist forces were under the command of Prince Alexander Sergeivich Menshikov, who had 40,000 men at his disposal. The Russians occupied an extremely strong position on hilly terrain south of the Alma. Menshikov divided his forces so that 26,000 men would face an equal number of British troops at the decisive point; his remaining men would be outnumbered by the French, but the latter were directed to an outflanking move that would take much time to execute. The British assault was to be crucial, which is why the wargame scenario is devoted to their efforts (an outline of the deployment of both armies is illustrated on the map provided below).

Menshikov had every reason to be confident, given the strength of his position. Unfortunately for the Russians, their army was woefully inadequate for the forthcoming task. In particular, leadership was appalling at all levels – Menshikov himself proved utterly incapable of coordinating his defence, whilst officers at lower levels were often promoted from the ranks and frequently barely literate. With these handicaps, it was inevitable that the Russian infantry in particular was poorly trained: it could only operate in column formation, proving incapable of mastering the intricacies of drill required to form a firing line, and, as a result, a musketry duel with enemy troops would inevitably prove decidedly one-sided. This was exacerbated by defective equipment; Russian infantry was still armed with smoothbore muskets, whereas both French and British troops had rifled small arms.

Not that the allies had it easy. The strength of the Russian position has already been noted, but both French and British armies had leadership problems of their own: units were frequently delayed through the failure to issue coherent orders. Further, the western forces seldom acted in a united manner: there was little communication between French and British, who often failed to inform each other what they were up to. The western troops were, however, excellent; their fighting qualities gave the most indifferent leaders a chance to succeed. This was especially true of the British infantry, whose ability to move and fight in line formation was astounding, and guaranteed to reap rich rewards.

The battle began when the French headed towards the Russian lines at 5.30am. Disorder ensued, resulting in the Gallic infantrymen halting for a coffee break. Once order was restored, the French progressed towards their objectives. Faced with this spectacle, Menshikov panicked. Despite being aware that the British assault would decide the battle, the Russian commander ordered all his reserves to the French sector, taking himself with them: he was therefore absent from the decisive arena as a result.

The British troops under Lord Raglan were meanwhile ordered to advance, which they did with a good deal of confusion, as all too many units got in the way of each other; Russian artillery fire from the Great Redoubt (occupied by units D and E in the wargame) added to the confusion. The British were however able to sort themselves out, and their forward progress was greatly facilitated by their Riflemen units (numbers 5, 6, and 7 in the wargame), whose skirmishing caused great discomfiture to the Russian troops. This enabled the Light Division (units 9, 10, and 11 in the wargame) to seize the Great Redoubt.

The Russians were far from finished, despite their extreme lack of coordination. An assortment of infantry units (represented by units C, F, M, and N) succeeded in driving the British back from the Great Redoubt. The Tsar's forces now had every prospect of winning the battle. At this point however, Lord Raglan himself took a hand in the proceedings. He had observed the British advance towards the Russian causeway artillery batteries (units G, H, and J), and noted that an eminence on the western end of the British advance, would provide an excellent position for a few artillery pieces to enfilade the Russian lines. Lord Raglan accordingly led his staff to the hilltop in question, and ordered an artillery battery to join them.

Raglan's staff had good reason to be concerned for their welfare at this point: the Russians could clearly see a group of British officers with their commander, all of whom were conspicuous by their chosen headgear of cocked hats, in the very midst of the Tsarist army's lines! Raglan's group undoubtedly presented a tempting target; but when the British guns arrived on the scene, it was the Russians who panicked (readers should note that the relevant unit is too small to be depicted on the wargame table: the effects of Lord Raglan's initiative are covered by a special rule). Many defending units were demoralised; all suffered from command paralysis. This coincided with the successful French assault upon their main objective of Telegraph Hill (so named because the Russians had set up a signalling station on the eminence in question). The British were then able to recapture the Great Redoubt, which precipitated a Russian retreat. Prince Menshikov's army had lost 5,700 men; the British suffered 2,000 casualties, whilst the French had losses of 1,350.

The allied victory was largely due to the conspicuous valour of the British infantry, combined with their superior firepower. Indifferent though much of the leadership was, it must be said that the frequently maligned Lord Raglan deserves great credit both for his personal bravery, and his vision in taking the initiative at a vital point in the battle.

The victory of the Alma was hard-won; the possibility of its being decisive was thrown away by poor leadership. The allies conspicuously failed to order a rapid advance on Sebastapol; they instead indulged upon a decidedly methodical approach march, losing the initiative as a result. The Russians were able to prepare for a lengthy siege thanks to the allied delay. Not that Menshikov's attempts to liberate Sebastapol fared any better; all failed, most notably in the notorious engagement at Balaclava. The western powers, who acquired additional support in the shape of a Piedmontese army, finally launched a successful assault upon Sebastapol on 8 September 1855.

The shambolic leadership all sides displayed during the Crimean War proved scandalous, especially in Britain. This was largely due to the efforts of the first serious war correspondent, William Howard Russell of *The Times*, whose despatches revealed the progress of the war in all its detail, from the heroism of the troops to the incompetence of their leaders – and, significantly, the appalling treatment of wounded soldiers. These unfortunates were shipped to the hospital at Scutari, on the Ottoman mainland, where the mortality rate reached forty-four percent. Russell's revelations inspired Florence Nightingale to do a great deal more than simply express indignation over the breakfast table. This remarkable woman launched a personal campaign to improve the medical care of the wounded troops, and headed for Scutari herself in order to resolve the problem. Nightingale's campaign met with remarkable success; by the time her mission was complete, the mortality rate at the infamous hospital had been reduced to just 2.5 per cent. Thanks to the efforts of William Russell and Florence Nightingale, war reporting and military hospitals were transformed beyond recognition.

So far as political events were concerned, peace was agreed in February 1856, and the subsequent Congress of Paris formulated a settlement. This had two major effects: firstly, the Black Sea was neutralised, thereby aborting Russian maritime intrigues; secondly, the Ottoman provinces of Moldavia, Wallachia and Serbia were effectively granted autonomy. However, the Ottoman Empire retained nominal authority over the provinces in question, which meant that they remained outside the clutches of the Russians.

Russia had lost a great deal of prestige in the Crimean War; her international authority and fearsome military reputation both lay in tatters, with three significant consequences. Firstly, the Tsarists were unable to launch any military adventures in the Balkans for another twenty years; secondly, the old autocratic and reactionary order lost so much prestige that it felt compelled to abolish serfdom in Russia, thereby liberating the peasantry from official slavery (albeit that the practical effects of the reform did little if anything to improve the erstwhile serfs' lot); and finally, Russian military impotence left her unable to continue propping up the old reactionary order in central Europe – thereby creating the opportunity for the reshaping of the continent with the creation of Italy and Germany.

THE WARGAME
Game Duration
The game lasts a total of 15 turns. The British player goes first in each turn.

Wargame Forces: The British Army
Lord Raglan's army is deployed on the table at the start of the game, as illustrated on the map provided.

Unit Type	Map Designation
Infantry (Elite, Rifled Musket, Close Order)	**1, 3, 9, 10, 11, 12, 13, 14**
Artillery (Smoothbore)	**2, 4, 8**
Skirmishers (Fanatic, Rifled Musket)	**5, 6, 7**

As already mentioned in the historical account, this wargame focuses on the British assault. Raglan's army is somewhat circumscribed by command difficulties, but benefits immensely from the ability of the British Infantry to march in Line formation (covered in the relevant special rule). The rifled muskets of the Infantry also give the British soldiery a huge advantage over their enemies. Lord Raglan's personal influence on the battle is also covered by a special rule.

The British army had some Cavalry units in the area, in the form of the Light Brigade. These were not deployed in the battle, but a military possibility allows the wargamer to see what might have happened had they materialised.

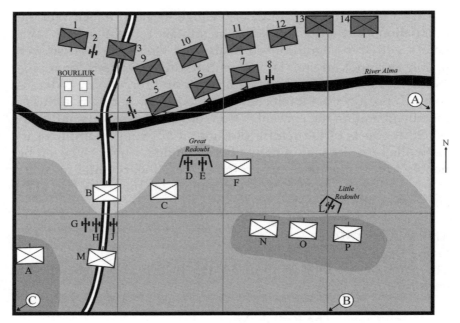

Map. 5. The Battle of the Alma

Wargame Forces: The Russian Army

Prince Menshikov's army is deployed on the table at the start of the game. Its positions are indicated on the map provided.

Unit Type	Map Designation
Infantry (Average, Smoothbore Musket, Close Order)	A, B, C, F, M, N, O, P
Artillery (Smoothbore)	D, E, G, H, J, L

The extremely sluggish nature of the Russian army is reflected in the special rule covering its terrible leadership. Its tactical deficiencies are reflected by not allowing any Skirmisher units to be deployed, and by a special rule preventing Infantry from operating in Line formation. The Russians must rely upon their plentiful Artillery, stubborn Infantry (see relevant special rule), and favourable terrain.

The Russians, like the British, had Cavalry units available, but failed to deploy them. A military possibility provides for their appearance.

Special Rules

(1) *British Drill.* British Infantry move in Line formation.

(2) *British Command Problems.* 1–3 Infantry or Artillery units of the British player's choice are out of command each turn (roll a die at the start of the British turn, rounding up any fractions). Affected units may neither move nor fire.

(3) *Raglan's Initiative.* Lord Raglan's foray towards the Russian lines had a significant impact upon the battle. Accordingly, whenever a British Infantry unit first moves within 12cm of the starting location of the Russian Causeway Batteries (units G, H, and J), Lord Raglan is assumed to be in close attendance. This has the following effects upon the Russians:

    (a) all Russian Infantry units must take a morale test.

    (b) No Russian unit of any type may move or fire in the subsequent Russian turn.

(4) *Russian Columns.* Russian Infantry may only operate in Column formation.

(5) *Stubborn Russian Infantry.* On the first occasion that a base is removed from a Russian Infantry unit as a result of enemy fire, the unit automatically passes the ensuing morale test.

(6) *Russian Leadership.* 1–6 Infantry or Artillery units of the Russian player's choice are out of command each turn (roll a die at the start of the Russian turn). Affected units may neither move nor fire.

(7) *Elevated Position.* To account for the Russian deployment on higher ground, Russian Infantry units always roll an additional die per base engaged in hand-to-hand combat.

(8) *The River Alma.* This watercourse is treated as a Stream.

(9) *The Great Redoubt.* 2 units may occupy this feature. They are treated as being within a Town.

(10) *The Little Redoubt.* A single unit can occupy this feature. It counts as being within a Town.

(11) *Bourliuk.* This village was set alight by the Russians before the British advanced. It is impassable to the troops of both sides.

Military Possibilities

(1) *Command Chaos.* After the number of units out of command has been determined according to special rules 2 or 6, the opposing player rolls a die. On a score of 5 or 6, he or she may decide which enemy Infantry or Artillery units are out of command.

(2) *Better Leadership.* Assume that either or both sides enjoyed a competent command structure. Ignore special rules 2 and/or 6.

(3) *His Blinkered Lordship.* Assume that Lord Raglan failed to seize his opportunity to exert personal influence upon the battle. Special rule 3 no longer applies.

(4) *French Failure.* The French attack fails. 1–3 Russian Infantry units (roll a die and halve the result, rounding up any fractions) appear at entry point C on turn 10.

(5) *French Triumph.* The French assault achieves meteoric success. 1–3 Russian Infantry units are immediately removed from the table at the start of turn 10 (they are assumed to have been directed to block the victorious French troops).

(6) *Better Russian Tactics.* This makes the highly unlikely suggestion that Russian Infantry could have been trained to fight in Line formation. Ignore the provisions of special rule 4.

(7) *British Cavalry.* The Light Brigade decides to put in an appearance. The British player rolls a die from the start of turn 10 onwards. On the first occasion he or she rolls a score of 5 or 6, 1–3 units of Cavalry (Elite) appear at entry point A (roll a die and halve the result, rounding up any fractions, to determine how many).

(8) *Russian Cavalry.* Menshikov's horsemen manage to rouse themselves. To account for the possibility of their arrival, the Russian player rolls a die from the start of turn 10 onwards. On the first occasion he or she rolls a 5 or a 6, 1–6 mounted units appear at entry point B (roll a die to determine how many). At least half the units must be Cossacks (Dragoons, Rabble, Smoothbore Muskets); the remainder may be Cavalry (Average).

Victory Conditions

Victory goes to the side with the greatest number of units occupying terrain above ground level at the end of turn 15. The British win if the number of units is equal.

Chapter 10

The Battle of Montebello (20 May 1859)

HISTORICAL ACCOUNT

The Battle of Montebello was the initial engagement of the Second Italian War of Independence, the genesis of which owed much to lessons learned from the abortive First War of Independence (1848–1849). The latter conflict was a united Italian effort, which foundered owing to the combined principalities' military inferiority: the standard of the troops was somewhat beneath that of their Austrian foes, and the Italian leadership lamentably beneath that of the octogenarian Austrian Field Marshal Radetzky (whose triumph led to Johann Strauss the Elder composing the celebrated 'Radetzky March' in the Field Marshal's honour).

Any attempt at achieving Italian liberation from Austrian hegemony needed to be orchestrated by the most formidable indigenous power, Piedmont, whose writ ran in north-western Italy. Fortunately for the Italian cause, Piedmont's chief minister Count Camillo di Cavour, was fully capable of rising to the challenge. Cavour realised that any bid for Piedmontese aggrandisement would need the assistance of a great European power. This was why Piedmont played an active military role in the Crimean War; doing so enabled her to win the admiration of her French and British allies. Conversely, Austria's neutrality during the Crimean imbroglio left her both friendless and distrusted.

By 1858 Cavour was ready to launch a diplomatic offensive, and his efforts found a sympathetic ear in France, in the person of Emperor Napoleon III. The latter had always been attracted by the cause of Italian independence, and was also conscious of the need to maintain the Bonaparte family image by achieving a spot of military glory and political aggrandisement. The Pact of Plombières agreed between France and Piedmont in July 1858, promised to achieve both. Its terms were that a successful Franco-Piedmontese war against Austria would lead to Piedmont ceding Nice and Savoy to France, whilst taking Lombardy and Venetia from the Hapsburgs. These territories would then combine with the duchies of Parma and Modena to form a new Kingdom of Upper Italy.

Unfortunately for the conspirators, they needed a casus belli – and the currently conciliatory Hapsburg governments in Lombardy and Venetia showed no signs of providing one, despite all of the prospective antagonists mobilising their armies. There was indeed every prospect that the Piedmontese would have to back down, since invading other states without an excuse was regarded as utterly deplorable in nineteenth-century Europe. However, the Austrian Foreign Minister, Graf Ferdinand von Buol-Schauenstein, promptly made the disastrous error of issuing an ultimatum to Piedmont on 22 April 1859, demanding that the Italian kingdom unilaterally demobilise her army. This provided an excuse for France and Piedmont to wage war against the Hapsburgs, which promptly broke out by the end of the month.

The folly of Buol's untimely belligerence was thrown into espe-cially sharp relief by the inadequacy of Hapsburg military leader-ship. Radetzky had died aged 91 in January 1858, and if he had still been in charge the Austrians might have won – for the late Field Marshal was still conducting manoeuvres the year before his death, and his military aptitude remained unaffected. His replacement was Field Marshal Gyulai, who was indecisive where Radetzky had been vigorous. As a result, the Hapsburg armies remained in Lombardy, rather than launching an offensive against Piedmont before the French could arrive to succour their ally. By May it was too late: the French had materialised, arriving with some rapidity owing to the transportation of their armies to Piedmont by rail and sea. By 20 May, the French advance guard was ready to engage the Austrians on the field of Montebello.

Most of the battlefield was a flat plain, whose most notable features were a series of vineyards, complete with irrigation canals. The former were lined with trees, which served to obstruct obser-vation for artillery units; the latter impeded the movement of the guns. As a result, ordnance played a limited role in the battle. The

114

new railway line was however to have an effect, and the village of Montebello itself, situated as it was upon higher ground, was the scene of much bitter fighting.

The French commander, General Forey, led about 8,000 men, whereas his Austrian opponent General Stadion commanded 20,000. The French were nevertheless concentrated, and the latter widely dispersed. Forey promptly launched a headlong attack at 2.00pm, and had driven the Austrians out of the hamlet of Genestrello (not depicted on the map; its location is marked by the Austrian Artillery unit 'B') an hour later. The Hapsburgs fell back on Montebello, which formed the focal point of their defence.

Stadion should have been able to handle the situation. He had plenty of troops available, the rapid arrival of which would have routed his enemy. However, Forey's aggression convinced Stadion that he was actually outnumbered by his foe, and the sluggish Hapsburg command structure ensured that their reinforcements arrived in a somewhat dilatory manner. For example, the Prince of Hessen's command (arriving at point 'C' on turn 3 of the wargame) was delayed by aggressive attacks against it from a numerically inferior force of French infantry and Piedmontese cavalry (arriving at point 'B' on turn 4). This was in contrast to the French, who moved with great rapidity: one startling innovation saw some of Forey's reinforcements use the railway to take troops onto the battlefield – the first time this had ever been done.

The French assaults on Montebello had meanwhile been ongoing, preceded by cavalry charges from their Piedmontese allies (unit number 6 in the wargame). These served to delay the arrival of Austrian reinforcements, allowing the French to take Montebello after some bitter fighting; the Hapsburgs being driven out by 6.00pm. Stadion promptly ordered a retreat; Forey's men were in no condition to pursue, but had nevertheless achieved a notable victory. The French had lost about 750 men; the Austrians approximately 1,400.

The battle of Montebello set the pattern for the entire war, with French improvisation, aggression and élan overcoming Austrian sluggishness and inertia. The later French victories at Magenta and Solferino owed everything to this tactical superiority – although on both sides strategic planning and generalship at the highest levels could most charitably be described as confused. Casualties were moreover very high at both engagements, which had two consequences. Firstly, the sight of blood staining the red breeches of the French infantry at Magenta led to the creation of the colour that now bears the name of the battle. The events at Solferino were to have more significant ramifications. For a Swiss businessman, Henri Dunant, was passing the battlefield and became appalled at the sight of the slaughter; however, unlike most people in a similar position, he actually decided to do something about it. Dunant convened the 1863 Geneva Conference, which led to the creation of the International Red Cross, and the writing of the Geneva Convention. The former has done more to ameliorate the consequences of warfare than any other organisation; the latter has been the only document to have any lasting effect upon making the waging of war less savage, establishing as it did the precedent for later Conventions which extended its remit.

The victories of Magenta and Solferino led to the capture of Lombardy, and the consequent Hapsburg retreat to Venetia. This province was however covered by the formidable fortresses of the Quadrilateral (Mantua, Peschiera, Verona, and Legnano). Faced with this obstacle, Napoleon III decided to secure his existing gains, and reached a peace deal with the Hapsburgs. The Piedmontese were furious: they had still ceded Nice and Savoy to France, but had only gained Lombardy from the Austrians. However, this partial success was to lead to something more substantial, as the central Italian duchies of Tuscany, Parma and Modena revolted against their pro-Hapsburg rulers. As a result, these duchies were to be added to Piedmontese jurisdiction.

The most remarkable development of the Second Italian War of Independence was now to occur. For men like Cavour had no particular desire to unite the whole of Italy; their intention was to control the northern part of the peninsula whilst leaving the notoriously poor and corrupt Kingdom of Naples to its own devices. However, Cavour had not calculated for the role of the veteran revolutionary Guiseppe Garibaldi, who sought to exploit yet another of the frequent Sicilian revolts against the misrule of the Bourbon Neapolitans. His initial force comprised just a thousand men; these proceeded to rout their much larger opponents in Sicily. By September 1860 Garibaldi crossed over to the mainland and soon took Naples. As a result, Cavour had to act fast. His adroit diplomacy led to the Piedmontese army intercepting Garibaldi, and winning the latter's support for the inclusion of Naples and Sicily within the new kingdom of Italy (which was to become fully united following the inclusion of Venetia after Austria's defeat against Prussia in 1866, and the Papal territories after a brief conflict in 1870). Cavour died in 1861, and his fears concerning the difficulties of administering the poor and lawless south came to pass in the following decades. As for Garibaldi, the unification of Italy was all he wanted; refusing all honours from the new state, he retired to his island home in Caprera. Such a renunciation of financial gain was almost unique: as a result, Garibaldi acquired a moral stature that his singular selflessness undoubtedly deserved.

THE WARGAME
Game Duration
The game lasts a total of 15 turns. The France-Piedmontese player goes first in each turn.

Wargame Forces: The Franco-Piedmontese Army
General Forey's initial forces are deployed as indicated on the map provided. Their composition and status are outlined below:

Unit Type	Map Designation
French Infantry (Average, Rifled Musket, Loose Order)	4, 5
French Chasseurs (Elite, Rifled Musket, Loose Order)	2
French Skirmishers (Elite, Rifled Musket)	1
Piedmontese Cavalry (Elite)	6
French Artillery (Bronze Rifled)	3

The Franco-Piedmontese initial force outnumbers its Austrian opponents and must take advantage of this initial superiority in order to win the battle. It will be assisted in this by the provisions of the special rules, especially that covering the French shock attack doctrine: the willingness of the French Infantry to close to the point of the bayonet which overcame the ability of Hapsburg musketry to retard their progress.

117

Forey's army also has three contingents of reinforcements to consider. These arrive according to the schedule indicated below:

Turn of Arrival	Unit Type	Unit Designation	Entry Point
2	French Infantry (Average, Rifled Musket, Loose Order)	7, 8	A
2	French Artillery (Bronze Rifled)	9	A
4	French Infantry (Average, Rifled Musket, Loose Order)	10	B
4	Piedmontese Cavalry (Elite)	11	B
6	French Infantry (Average, Rifled Musket, Loose Order)	12, 13	A

Wargame Forces: The Austrian Army

General Stadion's initial force is arrayed on the map as outlined below:

Unit Type	Map Designation
Infantry (Average, Rifled Musket, Loose Order)	A, D, E
Skirmishers (Elite, Rifled Musket)	C
Artillery (Smoothbore)	B

The Austrian army depends largely upon the progress of its reinforcements to win the game, although its ability to do so is somewhat retarded by the limitations of its command structure, as stated in the special rules. The Hapsburgs' reinforcement schedule is outlined below:

Turn of Arrival	Unit Type	Unit Designation	Entry Point
2	Infantry (Average, Rifled Musket, Loose Order)	F, G	E
2	Artillery (Smoothbore)	H	E
3	Infantry (Average, Rifled Musket, Loose Order)	J, K	C
3	Skirmishers (Elite, Rifled Musket)	L	C
3	Artillery (Smoothbore)	M	C
4	Infantry (Average, Rifled Musket, Loose Order)	N	D
6	Infantry (Average, Rifled Musket, Loose Order)	O, P, Q	E
6	Artillery (Smoothbore)	R	E

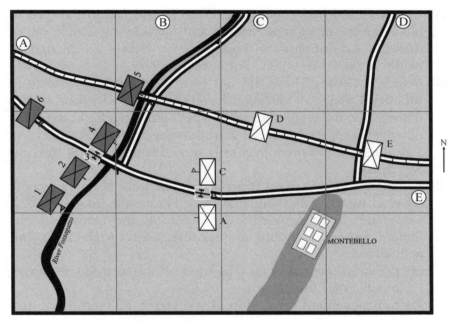

Map 6. The Battle of Montebello

Special Rules

(1) *French Elan.* French Infantry may always charge enemy Infantry units, irrespective of relative strength levels.

(2) *Austrian Inertia.* The Hapsburg leadership difficulties are accounted for by only allowing 33 per cent of Infantry and Artillery units on the table (fractions are always rounded up) to be in command. Units in command always function at full effectiveness; their less fortunate comrades are subject to the following restrictions:

(a) they move at half their normal speed.

(b) they only roll half their usual allocation of dice when firing during their own Firing phase (defensive fire during the enemy Charge Sequence is never penalised)

Players should note that Skirmisher units are always in command. So too are reinforcements, but only on the turn they enter the battle. The Austrian wargames general may always select precisely which of his or her units are in or out of command.

(3) *Vineyards.* The trees that lined these terrain features served to block the line of sight of Artillery units, rendering aiming rather difficult. Accordingly, all units in open terrain are treated as being under cover when shot at by Artillery.

(4) *Irrigation Canals.* These did not form a significant obstacle to Infantry, Cavalry or Skirmisher units, which is why they are not depicted on the wargames table. The many irrigation canals did however comprehensively retard the movement of Artillery. As a result, Artillery units may only move along roads or the railway track.

(5) *By Rail to Battle.* General Forey's audacious use of the railway is covered by the following rule. Any Franco-Piedmontese reinforcements arriving from entry point 'A' may move an unlimited distance along the railway line, subject to the following restrictions:

    (a) rail movement may only be used on the turn the reinforcements enter the game.

    (b) rail movement must stop at a distance of 18cm from any Austrian unit.

    (c) units may never combine rail and non-rail movement.

(6) *The Fossagazzo.* This insignificant obstacle is treated as a stream.

Military Possibilities

(1) *Radetzky Lives.* If Field Marshal Radetzky had survived long enough to take command in 1859 (or if the spirit he engendered had outlived his passing in 1858), the Hapsburg armies would have enjoyed decidedly better leadership. To account for this possibility, the Austrian Inertia rule no longer applies; all units are always assumed to be in command.

(2) *Divided Loyalties.* The Croats who had always made up a large proportion of Austrian Skirmisher units, had been decidedly sympathetic to Slav anti-Hapsburg agitation in 1848. Such disaffection can be simulated by reducing the morale of Austrian Skirmisher units to Average.

(3) *Austrian Cavalry.* Mounted units were present on the Hapsburg side at Montebello, but performed so ineffectively that they are not included in the wargame. Players who wish to allow them to appear may field 2 Austrian Cavalry units (both of which have

Average morale). One unit enters at Point 'C' on turn 3; the other at Point 'D' on turn 4.

(4) *Appalling Musketry.* The Hapsburgs paid little attention to fire-arms training in order to reduce the defence budget. However, their Lorenz rifled muskets were superior to their French counterparts, which is why I have not chosen to penalise Austrian firing: poor training is assumed to have been balanced by better weaponry. Players who wish to account for Hapsburg ineptitude always roll one fewer die than the level normally permitted when Infantry units are firing (subject to the proviso that at least one die is always rolled). Note that Skirmishers are not penalised; they did actually indulge in target practice.

Victory Conditions
The side that controls Montebello at the end of Turn 15 wins the game.

Chapter 11

The Battle of Oeversee
(6 February 1864)

HISTORICAL ACCOUNT

Denmark may not have been a major European power, but she was deeply embroiled in one of European diplomacy's most delicate issues. The 'Schleswig-Holstein Question', as it was known, was so notoriously convoluted and intractable that British Prime Minister Lord Palmerston once quipped that only three people could answer it: one (Prince Albert) was dead; the second (a German professor) went mad thinking about it; and the third (Palmerston himself) knew the answer once but had forgotten it now!

The intractability of the Schleswig-Holstein Question saw its genesis in a contradiction between legal and customary allegiance, and the ethnicity of the local population. For Schleswig and Holstein were two duchies occupying territory immediately south of Denmark; they had always enjoyed very close links with the latter kingdom, but were not part of Denmark itself – despite the fact that they were always ruled by members of the Danish royal family. Unfortunately for the prospects of peace, Holstein (the southernmost duchy) was largely German in ethnic identity, so much so that she was included within the German Confederation in 1815. There was also a substantial German population in southern Schleswig.

This rather heady mix of legal precedent and ethnic agitation had already led to one war in 1848, when Prussia supported the Germans in the duchies as the latter launched a bid for liberation (as they saw it) from Danish rule. The Prussian army of the time was not however of particularly high quality, and the Prussian monarchy was more intent upon re-establishing its authority over the liberal revolutionaries of the time than indulging in foreign adventures. As a consequence, the Danes were able to crush the rebellion in the duchies, which were restored to their previous position.

The Danish victory suited three great powers rather well. France, Russia and Britain were already under a treaty obligation (since 1727) to prevent non-Danish interference in the affairs of Schleswig and Holstein; more pertinently, none of the three signatories wanted any major power to control the entrance to the Baltic Sea, which would have happened if the duchies were governed by Prussia or Austria.

The international situation had changed somewhat by 1863. Russia had been gravely weakened as a consequence of the Crimean War, and was in no position to indulge in any foreign intervention; Napoleon III was sentimentally attached to the cause of German nationalism, as befitting what he saw as the Revolutionary and Napoleonic inheritance; and Britain had no intention of intervening anywhere without allies.

Unfortunately for the Danes, the death of King Frederick VII without a male heir in November 1863 brought the Schleswig-Holstein Question to the fore once again. For the precedent of 1460 dictated that the Salic Law (which we have already met in Chapter 7, and which dictated that succession to the relevant territory could only occur through a direct male bloodline) applied. This rather arcane precedent also stated that Schleswig and Holstein could never be divided politically. The new Danish King Christian IX was motivated more by logic than by custom however: his solution was to effectively annex Schleswig whilst leaving Holstein to its own devices. This may have been eminently sensible; it did however arouse the ire of German nationalists everywhere, who wanted to see both duchies form part of a Germanic polity.

Such agitation could have achieved nothing unaided. On this occasion however, it found a sympathetic hearing in both Austria and Prussia, despite the fact that neither monarchy had any sympathy for nationalistic sentiments. The Hapsburgs merely saw the dispute as a means to obtain continued primacy within the German Confederation. Prussian motives were more subtle. Her new Minister-President (Prime Minister), Otto von Bismarck, realised that his preferred model of authoritarian monarchism could only be secured with the support of liberals – and he was astute enough to realise that military glory would always win the allegiance of the Prussian subjects, whatever their nominal political allegiance.

123

Accordingly, Prussia and Austria were ready to wage war against Denmark; the conflict broke out in January 1864.

The Danes were fully aware of the difficulties of their strategic position, faced as they were by two major powers. It was evident that Holstein was completely indefensible, which was why the Danish army had withdrawn from the duchy in 1863. Schleswig was another matter: the Danes felt that they could make a stand at a line of fortifications known as the Danevirke, delaying the Austro-Prussian armies long enough for diplomatic intervention from the other great powers to play its part in ending the conflict. Unfortunately for Denmark, her army had just undergone a doubtless necessary but inevitably disruptive reorganisation. This created a temporary loss of effectiveness at the most untimely possible moment. The fact that the army had been conscripted since 1849 added to its problems: potential manpower may have been increased in theory, but the fact that many ethnic Germans from Schleswig had been recruited inevitably led to the risk of divided loyalties in the ranks. It has to be said that most Danish units behaved with great credit, especially when one considers that they were forced to fight against the odds; there were however occasional lapses under fire, which could have unfortunate effects.

The Danish plan was rendered null and void by the Austrian victory at the Battle of Jagel-Overselk on 3 February 1864. The Danish commander, General Christian Julius de Meza, realised that he could not counter the consequent threat to the Danevirke owing to the lack of sufficient numbers. De Meza accordingly ordered a retreat from the fortifications. The jubilant Austrians pursued with enthusiasm, catching up with the Danish rearguard north of Oeversee on 6 February.

The Austrian army at the time of the Second Schleswig War had greatly improved following its poor showing during the Second Italian War of Independence, just five years previously. The Hapsburgs had noted how effective the French infantry assaults had been, and proceeded to rely upon bayonet attacks themselves. These were now supported by much improved artillery. This had discarded its old smoothbore pieces and replaced them with more accurate rifled ordnance; moreover, these guns were no longer employed in reserve, where they could not respond to developments on the battlefield. The Austrian artillery was instead deployed in close support of the attacking infantry columns, giving the firepower that helped facilitate the effectiveness of bayonet assaults. The Hapsburgs were also blessed with excellent leadership in the person of Baron Leopold von Gablenz, who specialised in seizing the initiative rather than merely responding to the enemy.

The Danish rearguard occupied a good position on the battlefield of Oeversee, which was thoroughly covered with a blanket of snow. Its right flank was protected by Lake Sankelmark, which could not be successfully crossed by the enemy despite the fact that it was currently covered in ice. The Danish left flank was guarded by a wood, and a small hill in the rear allowed for the deployment of artillery (the positions of both Danish and Austrian forces are indicated on the wargame map provided). The Danes were undoubtedly shaken by their precipitate retreat, but they were fortunate in the forceful leadership provided by their commander Colonel Max Müller, who intended to make full use of the 3,000 men at his disposal. Müller was usually a great believer in the efficacy of bayonet assaults; such attacks were clearly inappropriate for a rearguard, but its commander's conspicuous personal leadership did much to steady the ranks of his men.

Gablenz's pursuing force of approximately 4,500 men started to arrive on the scene from 3.00pm, with the 9th Hussar cavalry regiment being first to arrive, together with six artillery pieces (which far outgunned the Danes, who had just two guns at their disposal). Gablenz ordered an immediate charge, in the hope that his foes would promptly run away: they did not, and the Austrian cavalry was repulsed. The Hapsburg artillery was much more effective however; its Danish counterpart was soon driven off, and the enemy infantry began to suffer in turn.

Müller's difficulties were exacerbated further when the Austrian infantry arrived in numbers at 4.00pm. Gablenz not only ordered a frontal assault, but also sent some of his units around the Danish left in the vicinity of the wood. The use of flanking attacks was something of a speciality where Gablenz was concerned: it was by no means a feature of his fellow Hapsburg commanders, whose penchant for the frontal assault was to have unfortunate consequences in later wars.

The Austrian pressure on the Danish army forced Müller to order a retreat from his position. His troops had suffered serious casualties, but he could be said to have succeeded in his mission; the main Danish army was able to retreat in good order rather than run away in a precipitate rout. It retired to its last remaining foothold in Schleswig, the Duppel fortifications and the island of Als.

THE WARGAME
Game Duration
The game lasts a total of 10 turns. The Austrian player goes first in each turn.

Wargame Forces: The Austrian Army
Baron Gablenz's initial force is deployed as indicated on the map. Its composition and status is outlined below:

Unit Type	Map Designation
9th Hussars Cavalry (Average)	1
Artillery (Bronze Rifled)	2, 3

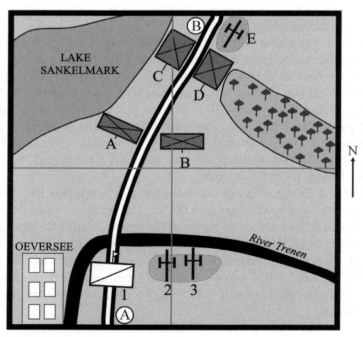

Map 7. The Battle of Oeversee

Oeversee was a rather small battle, which is why it can be simulated as a minigame on a small table, and with a length of just 10 turns. Gablenz's army was a thoroughly solid and well led force; the bayonet assault doctrine of its Infantry rendered it especially formidable when opposed by rifled muskets. Its effects are considered in the relevant Special Rule.

Most of the Austrian army arrives as reinforcements, according to the schedule indicated below:

Turn of Arrival	Unit Type	Unit Designation	Entry Point
1	Jäger Infantry (Elite, Rifled Musket, Loose Order)	4	A
1	Skirmishers (Elite, Rifled Musket)	5	A
2	Infantry (Average, Rifled Musket, Loose Order)	6	A
3	Infantry (Average, Rifled Musket, Loose Order)	7, 8	A

The Jägers are best treated as an élite Infantry unit with an additional Skirmisher element, rather than operating entirely in open order. This reflects their mode of operation.

Wargame Forces: The Danish Army

Colonel Müller's rearguard is deployed as illustrated on the map. The classification of its constituent elements is indicated below:

Unit Type	Map Designation
Infantry (Levy, Rifled Musket, Loose Order)	A, B, C, D
Artillery (Bronze Rifled)	E

The disrupted nature of the retreating Danes is reflected by giving their Infantry a morale rating of Levy. This may seem harsh, but it does reflect the situation where a high proportion of Danish casualties were prisoners; and also for the extraordinary behaviour of one regimental commander who escorted a wounded fellow officer to the rear, rather than lead his unit as he should have done. The role of Colonel Müller's personal leadership in helping morale is covered by a Special Rule however; and those who believe my classification of the Danish Infantry is both harsh and unreasonable can use the relevant Military Possibility.

The Danish Artillery was extremely weak, its commander having just two guns at his disposal. This is covered in the relevant Special Rule. More guns had been promised to Müller, but they never arrived – and neither did the other reinforcements he was expecting. The possibility of their appearance is covered in one of the Military Possibilities.

Wargamers should note that Infantry units C and D (comprising the 11th Danish Regiment) deploy in Column formation at the start of the game.

Special Rules
(1) *Bayonets of the Empire.* Austrian Infantry units must remain in Column formation throughout the game. They may however always charge enemy Infantry units, irrespective of relative casualty levels.

(2) *Max Müller.* The Colonel's personal leadership is accounted for by allowing the Danish player to nominate a single Infantry unit at the start of each turn. That unit sees its morale raised to Elite for the remainder of that turn.

(3) *Danish Artillery.* This weakened unit only rolls 2 dice when it fires. It is also eliminated upon the acquisition of just 2 hits, rather than the usual 4.

(4) *Waterways.* Lake Sankelmark is impassable; the River Trenen is treated as a stream.

Military Possibilities
(1) *Danish Commitment.* This rule allows for the arrival of the units that had been promised to Colonel Müller, but never materialised. They appear according to the schedule indicated below:

Turn of Arrival	Unit Type	Unit Designation	Entry Point
3	Artillery (Bronze Rifled)	F	B
3	Infantry (Levy, Rifled Musket, Loose Order)	G	B

Players should note that the Artillery reinforcement (unit F) is at full strength, unlike that which was deployed initially (unit E).

(2) *Danish Morale.* It could be argued that the Danish Infantry have been rated rather harshly. As a more favourable alternative,

128

1–3 Infantry units (roll a die and halve the result, rounding up any fractions) are reclassified as enjoying Average morale.

(3) *Thrusting Hapsburgs*. Gablenz was hoping that his initial cavalry charge would seriously undermine the morale of the Danish rearguard. To account for this possibility, if the 9th Hussars charge any unit at all during the first 2 Austrian turns, all Danish units must immediately test morale.

Victory Conditions

The Austrian player wins if no Danish units are within 12cm of the road running between entry points 'A' and 'B' by the end of turn 10. Failure to do so results in a Danish victory.

Chapter 12

The Battle of Rackebull
(17 March 1864)

HISTORICAL ACCOUNT

Following their success in driving the Danish army from the Danevirke, the Austrian army temporarily took a back seat in the war. The task of assaulting the Duppel fortifications was now left to the Prussian army. This was a long way short of the all-conquering force it was to become in 1866 and 1870: the early stages of the Second Schleswig War had seen a humiliating reverse against the Danes at the Battle of Missunde, and the chastened Prussians were forced to learn from their mistakes. They soon proved themselves able to do so; the reforms implemented at the start of the 1860s had germinated the seeds of efficiency for which the Prussian army was to become justly renowned in the years ahead. By March 1864, the Prussian 1st Corps under Prince Friedrich Carl had captured the outlying positions of Duppel, Rackebull, and Rackebull Wood, and was preparing to invest the Duppel forts themselves.

The Danish government looked upon these unwelcome developments with a sense of shame. General de Meza had been removed from his post for abandoning the Danevirke. The government now proceeded to put pressure upon his successor, General Gerlach, to display rather more offensive intent. Gerlach's position was scarcely an enviable one: he was fully aware that the numerical odds against him were rather unfavourable. He did however enjoy a temporary superiority; there were approximately 8,000 Danish troops in the general area of the forts, as compared with around 6,000 Prussians. As a consequence, Gerlach felt that a reconnaissance in force was feasible; he ordered his troops to recapture Duppel, Rackebull, and Rackebull Wood. Gerlach was however worried about the likely consequences of a pitched battle, and simultaneously ordered his local commanders to avoid a sustained engagement. These rather contradictory orders were to engender much confusion.

The battlefield itself was largely flat, although the countryside was covered by knicks (earthen banks topped with hedges), which served both to slow down movement and provide cover from small arms fire. The Danes were able to traverse these obstacles and take the three objectives with few losses on the morning of 17 March.

Gerlach was pleased with these developments, and proceeded to order a partial withdrawal (the situation at this point is illustrated on the map provided). Unfortunately for the Danes, the Prussians had no intention of taking this lying down. The local commander of the latter army, General von Goeben, became convinced that he faced a major Danish offensive, and ordered a counterattack. This proved successful, as the Danes were driven from the Rackebull area.

The situation was now to become extremely confused, for von Goeben believed that his job was done and promptly ordered a partial withdrawal of his own. This however coincided with the arrival of more Danish troops in the area, and a protracted clash around Gerlach's original three objectives ensued. The fighting was ultimately to see the defeat of the Danes, and their withdrawal to the Duppel fortifications.

The engagement was chiefly notable for the tactical superiority displayed by the breechloading Dreyse needle gun, which was the weapon used by the Prussian infantry. It proved itself capable of destroying the Danish assault columns, and was largely responsible for the disparity in casualties: the Danes lost 680 men killed, wounded or taken prisoner, compared with 140 Prussians. The Battle of Rackebull also showed the new efficiency of the Prussian command structure: it was certainly true that neither of the opposing generals covered themselves in glory, but the Prussians were capable of committing far more of their men to the battle than their Danish opponents. The latter were accordingly utterly unable to exploit their temporary local superiority, and lost the battle as a result.

The aftermath of the Battle of Rackebull saw the Prussians invest and finally take the Duppel fortifications during the following month. The Danes were able to maintain a toehold in Schleswig by retreating to the island of Als; this too was lost after a Prussian

131

amphibious assault on 29 June. The subsequent allied invasion of Danish territory itself led to the capitulation of Denmark, and the signing of the Peace of Vienna on 30 October 1864. The terms of the document provided for Schleswig and Holstein being jointly administered by the victorious allies. As we shall see in the next chapter, however, Austria and Prussia were not destined to enjoy a harmonious relationship: both powers wished to dominate German affairs, and the events of the Seven Weeks War were to determine which state ended up in control of Germany.

THE WARGAME
Game Duration
The game lasts a total of 15 turns. The Prussian player goes first in each turn.

Wargame Forces: The Prussian Army
Prince Friedrich Carl's initial forces are set out on the map as indicated. Their troop types and classifications are shown below:

Unit Type	Map Designation
Skirmishers (Elite, Early Breechloading Rifle)	1
Infantry (Average, Early Breechloading Rifle, Loose Order)	2, 3, 4, 5
Artillery (Smoothbore)	6

The game starts just after the initial Danish attack had captured Duppel, Rackebull, and Rackebull Wood. The Prussians are poised to grasp the initiative, which is why they take the first turn.

The general improvement in Prussian military ability since the start of the campaign has been reflected in giving all troops steady morale. The standard scenario makes no attempt to reproduce the somewhat confused progress of the battle: for those who wish to simulate the slightly incoherent stream of contradictory orders prevalent on the day, the relevant Military Possibility can be used. Readers who do so should try to enter into the spirit of the game and maintain an aggressive posture when the troops are available: waiting for an enforced enemy withdrawal, only to launch an all-out attack enjoying overwhelming superiority with two or three turns

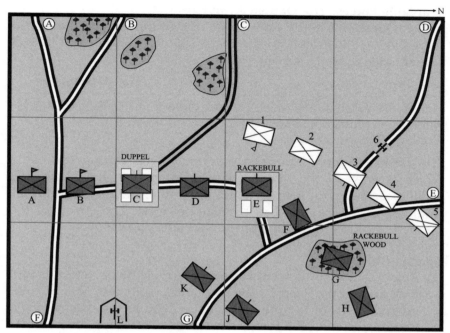

Map 8. The Battle of Rackebull

left, can win the game; it does not however reflect the historical situation.

The majority of the Prussian army enters the game as reinforcements; its entry schedule is indicated below:

Turn of Arrival	Unit Type	Unit Designation	Entry Point
1	Infantry (Average, Early Breechloading Rifle, Loose Order)	7, 8	B
1	Skirmishers (Elite, Early Breechloading Rifle)	9	B
1	Artillery (Smoothbore)	10	B
1	Infantry (Average, Early Breechloading Rifle, Loose Order)	11, 12	C
1	Skirmishers (Elite, Early Breechloading Rifle)	13	C
1	Artillery (Smoothbore)	14	C
8	Infantry (Average, Early Breechloading Rifle, Loose Order)	15	A
8	Skirmishers (Elite, Early Breechloading Rifle)	16	A

Wargame Forces: The Danish Army
General Gerlach's entire army is set out on the table at the start of the game, as illustrated on the map. The classifications of its constituent elements are set out below:

Unit Type	Map Designation
Infantry (Average, Rifled Musket, Loose Order)	C, D, E, F, G, H, K, J
Skirmishers (Elite, Rifled Musket)	A, B
Artillery (See Special Rule)	L

The Danish Army performed extremely well during the battle, which is why all the troops enjoy solid morale. It had no field artillery present, but instead relied upon intermittent contributions from the ordnance based in the Duppel forts. The effects of this gunnery are covered in one of the Special Rules below.

Special Rules
(1) *Knicks*. These earthen banks bordered most fields, which is why they are not depicted on the wargames table; they would cover far too much of the miniature battlefield, to the extent of suspending most of the troop bases in mid air! They did however have a significant impact upon the battle, as outlined below:
  (a) *Restricted Movement*. Troops in open terrain have their movement rate reduced to 8cm. Note that Road Movement is unaffected.
  (b) *Partial Cover*. Troops in open terrain are treated as if they inhabit a wood or town when shot at by Infantry or Skirmishers. This cover bonus does not apply when engaged by Artillery.
(2) *Duppel Forts*. The ordnance of the Duppel Forts is depicted by the Danish unit 'L'. This is a generic model designed to depict the contribution of several dispersed fortress guns to the battle (strictly speaking, there is no reason to deploy a specific miniature since the Duppel forts are just off the Eastern edge of the wargames table: it does however look far more attractive than an anonymous marker). The effects of the fortress artillery are as follows:
  (a) *Static*. Unit L may never move.
  (b) *Invulnerable*. Unit L may not be attacked (either by fire or hand-to-hand combat) by the Prussians. This is because the

latter's army at Rackebull lacked the strength to take on the fortress, and because unit L represents several dispersed guns rather than a single objective.

(c) *Field of Fire.* Unit L enjoys a field of fire of 180°.

(d) *Number of Shots.* Every time unit L fires, the Danish player rolls a die; the result indicates the number of shots available. The shots can be allocated to different enemy units as desired. For example, if 6 shots are available, the Danes may direct 4 shots at one target, and 2 at a second.

(e) *Siege Guns.* The Duppel ordnance consisted of smoothbore pieces, but they were of large calibre. Unit L therefore has a range of 48cm.

Military Possibilities

(1) *Mixed Messages.* The confused orders issued during the battle are simulated by applying the following rules whenever Duppel, Rackebull, and Rackebull Wood are all occupied by friendly units:

(a) Leave one unit garrisoning each objective.

(b) Withdraw 4 other units from the battle. These must head for the nearest friendly entry point (points A, B, C, D and E for the Prussians; points F and G for the Danes) and exit the table.

(c) If the enemy captures any of the three objectives, the units that are currently retreating may stop retreating and fight as desired. Units that have already exited the table may return to the fray.

(2) *Danish Coordination.* This rule postulates what might have happened if the Danes had committed all available units to the battle. To simulate its possible effects, the Danish player may deploy the following reinforcements. They may enter at either of the designated entry points as desired:

Turn of Arrival	Unit Type	Unit Designation	Entry Point
8	Infantry (Average, Rifled Musket, Loose Order)	M, N	F or G
8	Skirmishers (Elite, Rifled Musket)	O	F or G

Victory Conditions

The Prussian player must control Duppel, Rackebull, and Rackebull Wood at the end of Turn 15, in order to achieve victory. If he or she fails to do so, the Danish player wins the game.

Chapter 13

The Battle of Nachod
(27 June 1866)

HISTORICAL ACCOUNT

The Second Schleswig War had turned out exceptionally well for Prussia, producing as it did an increase in her political prestige, and a marked improvement in her army's military competence. Its aftermath also showed that the alliance between Prussia and Austria was tenuous at best; for the problems of joint administration in the conquered duchies soon produced a rather hasty compromise in the shape of the Convention of Gastein (August 1865). This stipulated that Prussia would henceforth govern Schleswig, whereas the Austrians now controlled Holstein.

The real focus of tension did not however lie in minor administrative disputes. The underlying issue was over competing visions of Germany. So far as the Hapsburg Empire was concerned, the best approach was to maintain the status quo. Nor was this surprising: an imperial regime like the Austrian government was naturally and inevitably opposed to nationalism in any form – for its outbreak in any part of Europe would inevitably lead to demands for independence from national groupings within the Hapsburg Empire itself. The Austrians could moreover depend upon the support of many minor states within the geographical area of Germany, given that all these kingdoms were likely to either disappear or become enfeebled if a German national state was ever to be created. This explains why the Hapsburgs were to win the active (if not always effective) military support of Hanover, Bavaria, Saxony, Württemberg, Baden, Hesse-Darmstadt, Hesse-Cassel, and Nassau, when the Seven Weeks War eventually broke out in 1866.

The Prussian vision of Germany's future was rather more nuanced than that of their Hapsburg rivals. It was certainly true that the Prussian aristocratic ruling class, the Junkers, generally disliked nationalist agitation, regarding it as the vulgar preserve of bourgeois parvenus. The Prussian monarchy and government did however detest liberalism, whereas they merely disliked nationalism; and as observed in Chapter 1, the latter had the merit of being useful to both appease and neutralise the former ideology. For German liberals were generally extremely nationalistic in addition: they were therefore willing to acquiesce in a powerful monarchy, provided that the King of Prussia was willing to promote German nationhood.

The idea of achieving glory by military conquest was also entirely in keeping with Prussian tradition. For Prussia was originally a poor and insignificant part of eastern Germany: this all changed during the eighteenth century, when the creation of a military state under the strategic colossus that was King Frederick the Great converted Prussia into a great power. The renewed growth of the army from 1860 onwards (a trend examined in Chapter 1) served to revive memories of Prussian glory, and gave the sense of a whole new mission. For Germany could now be united thanks to the power of the Prussian army: and more pertinently for the Junkers, any new state could be ruled by the Prussian monarchy. In this way, tradition and nationalism could merge; and liberalism would be reduced from a dire political threat into an impotent and despised cheerleader.

It was now left for Otto von Bismarck to weave his diplomatic magic, since Prussia needed allies – or at least the neutrality of other European powers. This was all a matter of timing; and no statesman was more adept at seizing the moment than Bismarck. He was aware that Russia was still licking her wounds after the Crimean War, and was therefore both unable and unwilling to intervene in other European quarrels. France was also going through a period of weakness; and Britain would never interfere without the assistance of other great powers. The neutrality of these great nations was consequently assured.

Bismarck was to achieve far more than this with the new Kingdom of Italy. He was able to win an Italian alliance by promising the cession of Venetia from Hapsburg rule in the event of a successful military campaign. This alliance forced Austria into a war on two fronts, thereby stretching her resources.

A plausible *casus belli* was all that was now required. It materialised in June 1866 over the entirely predictable flashpoint of the erstwhile Danish duchies. Prussia argued that political refugees from Schleswig were being sheltered by the Austrians in Holstein; the Prussian army accordingly invaded the latter territory, and a war for the control of Germany inevitably followed.

The Seven Weeks War, as it was to become known, was fought in three separate theatres. The first of these was Italy, where Prussia's allies invaded Venetia. It has to be said that the Italian army did not get very far: it was defeated at the Battle of Custoza on 26 June. This rather inglorious effort was not however without benefits for the Prussian cause. For the Austrian army in Italy was not only removed from intervening elsewhere but, in a piece of truly spectacular misjudgement, the Hapsburg Emperor Franz Joseph appointed his best general, Archduke Albrecht, to command in the subordinate arena.

On the subject of secondary theatres, the next front opened up in western Germany, where the Prussian Army of the Main under General Eduard Vogel von Falckenstein was assigned the task of engaging and destroying Austria's minor German allies (this sphere of operations will be considered in the next chapter).

The decisive conflict was to be fought in Bohemia, where the Prussian 1st Army, 2nd Army, and the Army of the Elbe, all under the overall command of General Helmuth von Moltke, were to converge upon the Austrian Army of the North under General Ludwig von Benedek. The ensuing battle would settle the outcome of the entire war.

Moltke's operations were however fraught with difficulty, as his three attacking armies had to traverse separate mountain passes in order to gain access to Bohemia. This provided an excellent opportunity for Benedek to exploit his central position in the classic Napoleonic manner: the Army of the North could in theory have concentrated its strength and destroyed at least one Prussian army before its comrades arrived on the scene.

Unfortunately for the Hapsburgs, there was a dissonance between theoretical potential and factual reality. Moltke's plan would undoubtedly have proved fatal in Napoleonic times: the Prussian commander had however unilaterally changed the rules. For Moltke realised that the new reformed Prussian army could achieve feats that its predecessor could not: it could mobilise rapidly; it could move with equal speed thanks to the Prussian railway network, which was deliberately constructed with the needs of the army in mind; and, most crucially of all, Moltke had helped to forge a group of staff officers whose execution of orders was to become almost legendarily efficient.

It was clear that the Army of the North would have to move with great speed if any of the Prussian forces were to be intercepted. Unfortunately for the Hapsburgs, Benedek may have been renowned for his personal bravery, which was the main reason he had been appointed; he was however notoriously inept at staffwork, and was moreover an appalling strategist. Benedek was in the singularly unfortunate position of being a brave and dedicated soldier who had been promoted far above his level of competence. As a consequence, the Army of the North was never able to mobilise or manoeuvre with the necessary expedition or efficiency.

Benedek's strategic ineptitude meant that the majority of opportunities were lost. The only real chance to inflict damage occurred on the eastern front, where the two separate corps of Generals Leopold von Gablenz and Wilhelm von Ramming, were in a position to attack contingents of Crown Prince Friedrich Wilhelm's 2nd Prussian Army. Both commanders fought battles on 27th June, and Gablenz was victorious at Trautenau. If Ramming could defeat General Karl von Steinmetz's 5th Prussian Corps at Nachod, then the 2nd Army would have been forced into retreat, thereby imperilling Moltke's grand strategic design.

Ramming certainly had numbers on his side. His 6th Austrian Corps had 33,000 men available, whereas Steinmetz only had 24,000 at his disposal. Unfortunately for the Hapsburgs, poor staffwork again took its toll upon their plans. A stream of contradictory orders and inadequate preparation led to Ramming's units arriving in a piecemeal manner, after some hasty forced marches. The Austrian troops were both disorganised and exhausted as a result. Despite this, they were willing to attack their foe. For the Hapsburgs had seen the success of assault columns in the Second Schleswig War, and were convinced that bayonet attacks would rout the Prussians as they had the Danes. Unfortunately for the Austrians, they failed to realise that whereas the Danish infantry was only equipped with muzzleloading rifled muskets, their new Prussian opponents were equipped with breechloading Dreyse needle guns. The latter rifle gave the Prussian infantry a rate of fire immeasurably superior to that which could be achieved with muzzleloading weapons: a fact which the Austrians were about to discover to their cost.

The battlefield of Nachod is illustrated on the map provided. Ramming's objective was to drive the Prussian advance guard (units A, B, C, and D) from its positions, occupying Wenzelberg, Wysokow, and the Wysokow Plateau in the process. A further drive would then take Altstadt, thereby bottling up the Prussians in the mountain pass behind Nachod. This would force a retreat, which would constitute a significant Austrian victory.

The battle began with a rash attack on Wenzelberg by General Hertwek's brigade (units 1, 2, and 3 on the map). This was repelled by the Prussian defenders, the effect of whose musketry came as a dreadful shock to the Hapsburg assault troops. Hertwek had to rely on General Jonak's men (the reinforcements arriving on turn 2 of the wargame) to have any impact whatsoever. The Austrian attacks only had any lasting effect when Ramming ordered his remaining troops (those arriving from Turn 5 of the wargame onwards) to launch a flanking attack through Wysokow. Sheer weight of numbers forced the Prussians back towards the Branka Wood, and Ramming sent his cavalry forward in what he thought would be the pursuit of a beaten foe.

Unfortunately for the Hapsburgs, the Prussians were far from finished. Steinmetz had ordered reinforcements forward, all of which were fresh and ready for the fray – a consequence of efficient staffwork. The Austrian failures in this area were about to play their baleful part in the battle; for Ramming's troops were now utterly spent as a result of their exertions: the Hapsburg horsemen were repelled by their Prussian counterparts, and the combined effects of the needle gun and some supporting artillery fire drove the Austrians back. Ramming was forced to order a general retreat; his force had suffered 7,500 casualties, whereas Steinmetz had only lost 1,100.

The Battle of Nachod encapsulated the Seven Weeks War on the Bohemian front, showing as it did what happened when faulty Austrian staffwork led to a loss of initiative. Ramming's failure at Nachod can be profitably contrasted with Gablenz's success at Trautenau: the latter general's flank attack was organised whereas the former's was improvised; and where Ramming failed, Gablenz

141

succeeded. Both Nachod and Trautenau did however demonstrate the terrible effects of the Prussian needle gun – the casualty figures at Nachod have already been mentioned, but even Gablenz's victorious army suffered four times as many casualties as their defeated Prussian opponents.

The failure at Nachod enabled the Prussian 2nd Army to combine with its compatriots on the battlefield at Königgrätz on 3 July. Benedek planned to fight a defensive engagement on this occasion, relying on musketry from prepared positions and the decidedly superior Austrian artillery. These tactics did moreover meet with a degree of success; however, superior Prussian organisation and inferior Austrian leadership played their part. For the 2nd Prussian Army arrived on the Austrian right wing at precisely the time that part of the latter, unable to resist temptation any longer, launched a bayonet assault on the Prussians to their front. The consequences of both these developments were entirely predictable, as the effects of the needle gun and the outflanking move forced an Austrian retreat. The Battle of Königgrätz was lost, along with the war itself – an inevitable consequence of Prussian technical, tactical and strategic superiority. The fate of Germany was also decided; her future now lay in the hands of Prussia.

THE WARGAME
Game Duration
The game lasts a total of 15 turns. The Austrians go first in each turn.

Wargame Forces: The Austrian Army
General von Ramming's initial force is deployed on the map as illustrated. Its classification is outlined below:

Unit Type	Map Designation
Infantry (Average, Rifled Musket, Loose Order)	1, 2
Skirmishers (Elite, Rifled Musket)	3

The Hapsburg reliance upon assault tactics is reflected in the 'Bayonets of the Empire' special rule. This has already been seen in Chapter 10; its effects when used against the needle gun are unlikely to be so successful. Wargamers who wish to consider how the Austrians might have performed with a tactical doctrine based upon

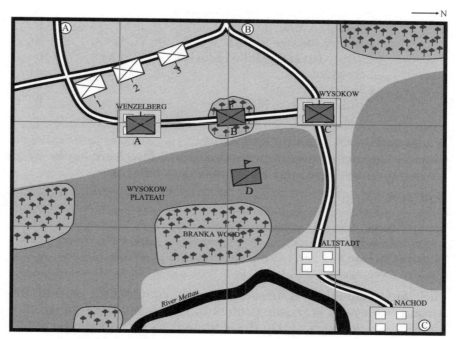

Map 9. The Battle of Nachod

firepower rather that shock, can experiment with the relevant military possibility.

Ramming's army is somewhat circumscribed by the special rule covering its exhaustion. The effects of this may seem harsh, but they do reflect the difficulties created by the shambolic Austrian command structure. Again, a military possibility provides for better leadership.

Most of the Hapsburg units enter the game as reinforcements, the schedule of which is stated below:

Turn of Arrival	Unit Type	Unit Designation	Entry Point
2	Infantry (Average, Rifled Musket, Loose Order)	4, 5	A
2	Artillery (Bronze Rifled)	6	A
5	Infantry (Average, Rifled Musket, Loose Order)	7, 8	A

5	Skirmishers (Elite, Rifled Musket)	9	A
5	Cavalry (Average)	10	B
6	Artillery (Bronze Rifled)	11, 12	B
7	Infantry (Average, Rifled Musket, Loose Order)	13, 14	B
7	Cavalry (Average)	15, 16	B
7	Artillery (Bronze Rifled)	17	B

Wargame Forces: The Prussian Army

General von Steinmetz's rather sparse initial forces are deployed as indicated on the map, and are classified as follows:

Unit Type	Map Designation
Infantry (Elite, Early Breechloading Rifle, Loose Order)	A, C
Skirmishers (Fanatic, Early Breechloading Rifle)	B
Cavalry (Average)	D

The improvement in Prussian infantry competence during the Second Schleswig War was profound, and is reflected by its very high morale rating. Cavalry development seems to have been less pronounced: I believe that its good performance at Nachod can be explained more by Austrian exhaustion than Prussian competence. Military possibilities are provided for wargamers who think differently: one of these provides for an enhanced shock capability for the Uhlan (Lancer) unit; another allows for the Dragoon unit to operate as such rather than as pure cavalry.

One aspect that must be considered is the faulty Prussian artillery doctrine of the time. The gunners were appalled at the prospect of losing their ordnance to the enemy, the ignominy of which was regarded as an appalling disgrace. They were unable to use their guns with any great effectiveness as a result – in particular, the new Krupp steel breechloading weapons were rendered null and void by the aversion to take risks with their deployment. This deficiency is covered by the relevant special rule; a military possibility provides for a more astute doctrine to prevail if desired.

Most Prussian units arrive as reinforcements, the schedule for which is stated below:

Turn of Arrival	Unit Type	Unit Designation	Entry Point
5	Cavalry (Average)	E	C
5	Artillery (Smoothbore)	F	C
6	Infantry (Elite, Early Breechloading Rifle, Loose Order)	G, H	C
6	Artillery (Smoothbore)	J, K	C
7	Infantry (Elite, Early Breechloading Rifle, Loose Order)	L, M	C
7	Skirmishers (Fanatic, Early Breechloading Rifle)	N	C
8	Artillery (Smoothbore)	O, P	C

Special Rules

(1) *Bayonets of the Empire.* Austrian Infantry units must remain in Column formation throughout the game. They may however always charge enemy Infantry units, irrespective of relative casualty levels.

(2) *Lorenz Rifle.* This weapon equipped the Austrian Infantry and Skirmisher units, and seems to have been more effective than most rifled muskets. Austrian Infantry and Skirmisher units may accordingly roll one additional die in total (not one additional die per base) whenever they fire.

(3) *Austrian Exhaustion.* All Hapsburg units are exhausted at the start of Turn 8. At the start of Turn 9, the Prussian player rolls a die, and halves the result, rounding up any fractions: the result indicates the number of turns for which Austrian units are exhausted. (Example: the Prussian player rolls a '3'; this is halved to 1½, and rounded up to 2. As a consequence, the Austrian army remains exhausted during turns 9 and 10.) The effects of exhaustion are as follows:

(a) units may only move at half their normal speed.

(b) no unit may charge the enemy.

(c) units only roll half their usual number of dice when firing (rounding up any fractions).

(d) Cavalry units only roll half their usual number of dice in hand-to-hand combat (rounding up any fractions).

(4) *Save the Guns!* Prussian Artillery units must retreat a full move whenever Austrian Infantry or Cavalry units move within 12cm.

(5) *River Mettau.* This watercourse may not be crossed.

Military Possibilities

(1) *Musketry of the Empire.* Players can see what would have happened if the Austrian Infantry relied upon fire rather than shock. To simulate this, the 'Bayonets of the Empire' rule no longer applies.

(2) *Hapsburg Horsemen.* The Austrian Cavalry enjoyed a very high reputation throughout Europe. Those who believe that such status was justified can reclassify all Austrian Cavalry units as having Elite morale.

(3) *Better Staffwork.* If the Hapsburgs had sorted out their command structure, their army would undoubtedly have performed much better. The effects of better leadership are as follows:

(a) the 'Austrian Exhaustion' rule no longer applies.

(b) all Austrian reinforcements arrive one turn sooner than scheduled.

(4) *Enlightened Artillery Doctrine.* The Prussian Artillery would have functioned much more effectively if it had been deployed with greater boldness. To see what would have happened if it had been, apply the following rules:

(a) units F, O, and P are reclassified as 'Steel Rifled' Artillery (they are now able to realise the potential of their new Krupp guns).

(b) the 'Save the Guns!' special rule no longer applies.

(5) *Prussian Dragoons.* These horsemen (represented by unit 'D') were trained to operate in a dismounted role, although they usually disdained such pedestrian (in every sense of the word) activity and operated as traditional Cavalry. The wargamer may however reclassify unit 'D' as Dragoons if desired (equipped with Early Breechloading Rifles).

(6) *Prussian Uhlans.* These troops (represented by unit 'E') performed rather well during the battle. I have assumed this to be a consequence of Hapsburg exhaustion rather than Prussian equestrian excellence; readers who disagree can allow unit 'E' to re-roll any dice scores that fail to register hits in hand-to-hand combat.

Victory Conditions

Wenzelberg, Wysokow and Altstadt must all be under the control of friendly units at the end of Turn 15. Any other result is a draw.

Chapter 14

The Battle of Kissingen (10 July 1866)

HISTORICAL ACCOUNT

Western Germany was both a political and a military backwater in 1866. As a consequence, when General von Moltke planned the Prussian campaign against Austria and her allies, he assigned relatively few troops to the region. The Army of the Main embodied a mere 50,000 men, which included some rather inferior Landwehr militia units. Its commander, General Eduard Vogel von Falckenstein, could moreover not be described as one of the brightest stars in the Prussian military firmament (albeit that he had a great conviction of his own excellence).

On the face of it, Moltke's plan appeared to suffer from hubris on a grand scale. For the Army of the Main had to face three enemy forces, which would vastly outnumber the Prussians if they were able to combine. The smallest of these foes was the Kingdom of Hanover, whose army of 20,000 was of extremely high quality, and well led at the tactical level by General von Arentschildt. Next came the Kingdom of Bavaria, whose field army boasted 50,000 men: it was however a somewhat unenthusiastic participant in the war, and was moreover commanded by Prince Carl of Bavaria – a man whose leadership skills were to prove woefully inadequate in the coming campaign. The third of the allied armies, a combined Federal corps, suffered from similar difficulties. Its 50,000 men included elements from Württemburg, Baden, Hesse-Darmstadt, Nassau, and even an Austrian contingent. Organising these disparate elements was a task far beyond their commander, Prince Alexander of Hesse.

Moltke was aware of the problem likely to afflict these widely dispersed foes – especially when their mobilisation arrangements were utterly shambolic. This chaos was completely alien to the

147

awesome efficiency displayed when the Prussians embodied and concentrated their forces, and Moltke realised that his smaller army was in a position to defeat its enemies one by one – despite his misgivings over the quality of von Falckenstein's leadership.

Events in Hanover soon served to confirm Moltke's thesis. For the Hanoverian army was not merely the smallest of the allied forces, it was also the most geographically northerly and hence the closest to the Prussians. Accordingly, the Hanoverians needed to mobilise rapidly in order to escape southwards and join their allies. This task proved to be beyond them, and the Army of the Main soon cut off the Hanoverian escape route. This was just as well for the Prussians, since von Falckenstein's own deficiencies led to a portion of his force becoming isolated and defeated in the ensuing Battle of Langensalza, fought on 27 June. This provided a graphic demonstration of the tactical potential of the Hanoverian army; unfortunately for von Arentschildt, his men may have won the battle, but they had also exhausted their supply of ammunition. As a result, the surrounded Hanoverians were forced to surrender to their Prussian foes.

Falckenstein's army then proceeded to move towards Fulda, in an attempt to prevent the juncture of the Bavarian and Federal armies. The latter proved especially slow to mobilise, and had not even gathered their full strength before their Bavarian allies were defeated by the Prussians at the Battle of Wiesenthal, fought on 4 July. This setback forced the Bavarians to retreat southwards to the River Saale; Prince Alexander's Federal corps meanwhile withdrew west towards Frankfurt.

Prince Carl's uncertain leadership resulted in the Bavarian army becoming both dispersed and disordered, and news of the Austrian defeat at Königgrätz only served to exacerbate Bavarian demoralisation. They were nevertheless still prepared to attempt to hold the line of the Saale, which precipitated the battle of Kissingen on 10 July.

The broad deployment of the respective antagonists can be seen on the map provided. The battle began when General von Goeben's Prussian division approached Kissingen, only to meet with stout resistance from the town's defenders. Unfortunately, Prince Carl had neglected to defend the demolished bridge south of Kissingen:

148

this omission was to prove costly, for the Prussians sent a substantial force to repair the bridge. As soon as Goeben's men were able to cross via the reconstituted bridge, the Prussians could launch a frontal and flanking assault upon Kissingen. Faced with this, the Bavarians were forced to retreat to Winkels early in the afternoon. A smaller Prussian force had meanwhile managed to repair another demolished bridge at the village of Friedrichshall (this settlement is too small to register as a town on the wargame map: its location is marked where the Bavarian Skirmisher unit 'C' is deployed), and proceeded to march upon Hausen. Both Winkels and Hausen fell soon afterwards, precipitating a Bavarian retreat.

General von Goeben believed that the battle was won, and ordered most of his men to retreat towards Kissingen in order to refit. This proved to be a serious miscalculation; the Bavarians were not yet ready to give up, and some reinforcements (arriving on Turn 10 of the wargame) proceeded to counter-attack the Prussians in Winkels from late afternoon onwards. Some bitter fighting followed, but the combination of defensive firepower from the Dreyse needle gun, and the arrival of Prussian reinforcements (those appearing on Turn 12 of the wargame) saved the day for Goeben's men. The Bavarians were forced to concede defeat; they had lost 1,300 men, whereas the Prussians had suffered 900 casualties.

The rest of the campaign in Western Germany followed what had become a familiar path, with the separated and poorly-led allied forces unable to combine effectively, leading to their eventual surrender. Both the Bavarian and Federal corps had fought hard on occasion; but poor leadership and ineffective mobilisation meant that they posed little ultimate threat to Falckenstein's Army of the Main. General von Moltke had always realised that Western Germany was a secondary theatre; he simply assigned enough troops to prevent the Federal German states combining with the main Hapsburg army.

The Seven Weeks War saw its formal conclusion with the signing of the Treaty of Prague on 23 August 1866. This document led to the creation of the North German Confederation, by which the previously independent indigenous states north of the River Main (Hanover, Hesse-Cassel, Nassau, Frankfurt and Schleswig-Holstein) were annexed by Prussia. Austria thereby lost her influence in German affairs. Her cession of Venetia to Italy meant that she also

149

lost her foothold in the latter country. The Hapsburgs were now forced to look southeastwards to the Balkans in order to wield any influence (which was to have decidedly unfortunate consequences in 1914, when her confrontation with Serbia precipitated the outbreak of the First World War).

The Treaty of Prague left the southern German states in a political limbo. Their strong separatist desires conflicted with economic imperatives, which determined ever closer ties with Prussia. They did however represent a potential source of instability so far as Prussia's chief minister, Otto von Bismarck, was concerned. He was absolutely determined that any French diplomatic arrangements with the southern German states could never come to fruition. Bismarck accordingly saw that any full, binding arrangement between northern and southern Germany might require another war; and as we shall see in the next chapter, this was to occur with France within four years.

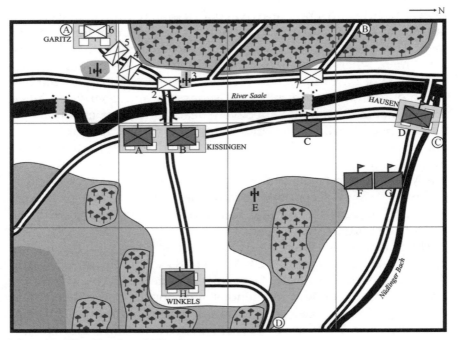

Map 10. The Battle of Kissingen

THE WARGAME
Game Duration
The game lasts a total of 15 turns. The Prussians go first in each turn.

Wargame Forces: The Prussian Army
General von Goeben's initial forces are deployed on the map as indicated. They are classified as follows:

Unit Type	Map Designation
Artillery (Smoothbore)	1, 3
Skirmishers (Elite, Early Breechloading Rifle)	2
Infantry (Average, Early Breechloading Rifle, Loose Order)	4, 5, 6, 7

The Prussian army will rely on the superiority of its needle guns, and its more flexible leadership, in order to prevail. Its higher morale status is also likely to have an effect. The peculiar circumstances created by the decision to withdraw following the initial Bavarian retreat, are covered in the military possibility examining 'Prussian Complacency'; the standard game is played without such convoluted arrangements.

The Prussian reinforcement schedule is indicated below:

Turn of Arrival	Unit Type	Unit Designation	Entry Point
4	Infantry (Average, Early Breechloading Rifle, Loose Order)	8	A
4	Cavalry (Average)	9	A
7	Infantry (Average, Early Breechloading Rifle, Loose Order)	10	B
7	Skirmishers (Elite, Early Breechloading Rifle)	11	B
7	Artillery (Smoothbore)	12	B
12	Infantry (Average, Early Breechloading Rifle, Loose Order)	13, 14, 15	A
12	Skirmishers (Elite, Early Breechloading Rifle)	16	A
12	Cavalry (Average)	17	A
12	Artillery (Smoothbore)	18	A

Wargame Forces: The Bavarian Army
Prince Carl's starting units are deployed on the map as indicated, and are classified as follows:

151

Unit Type	Map Designation
Infantry (Levy, Rifled Musket, Loose Order)	A, B, H
Skirmishers (Average, Rifled Musket)	C, D
Artillery (Smoothbore)	E
Cavalry (Levy)	F, G

I have assumed that the Bavarian army was fundamentally un-enthusiastic about fighting fellow Germans, and that they were also demoralised by Prince Carl's rather eccentric leadership, which explains the low morale rating of all units (a military possibility examines what might have happened had the Bavarians been blessed with a competent general). Prince Carl's indecision is reflected by the rather draconian restrictions upon movement and firing; however, I have given the Bavarians a bonus by allowing them the use of a unit of Steel Rifled Artillery (unit 'L' arriving on Turn 6). The Bavarians had just received a consignment of Krupp steel guns by 1866, and seem to have used these quite effectively; readers who believe that my classification of unit 'L' is excessively charitable are of course free to regard it as being equipped with smoothbore weapons. I have also allowed for the upgrading of some Bavarian units, on the basis that their *esprit de corps* must have been quite strong simply to continue fighting effectively, given the vicissitudes of the campaign.

The Bavarian reinforcement schedule is indicated below:

Turn of Arrival	Unit Type	Unit Designation	Entry Point
3	Infantry (Levy, Rifled Musket, Loose Order)	J	D
6	Infantry (Levy, Rifled Musket, Loose Order)	K	C
6	Artillery (Steel Rifled)	L	C
10	Infantry (Levy, Rifled Musket, Loose Order)	M, N	D
10	Skirmishers (Average, Rifled Musket)	O	D
10	Artillery (Smoothbore)	P	D

Special Rules

(1) *Goeben's Veterans.* General von Goeben's division became a highly efficient unit during the campaign in Western Germany. To account for this, 1–6 units (roll a die to determine how many) of the Prussian player's choice are upgraded by one morale class (for example, Infantry units can be upgraded from 'Average' to 'Elite'). These units are always designated at the start of the game.

(2) *Save the Guns!* Prussian artillerymen regarded the loss of their ordnance as an appalling humiliation. Prussian Artillery units must therefore retreat a full move whenever Bavarian Infantry or Cavalry units move within 12cm.

(3) *Royal Vacillation.* Prince Carl's indecisive leadership is accounted for by the following rule. Only 25 per cent of all Bavarian units currently on the table are in command (fractions are always rounded up; the Bavarian player may always decide precisely which units are in command at the start of each turn). Units that are in command move and fire as normal; units that are out of command suffer the following restrictions:

    (a) their movement rate is halved.

    (b) they only roll half their normal number of permitted dice, when firing during their own move (defensive fire against charging enemy units is not penalised).

(4) *Survival of the Fittest.* Some of the Bavarian units showed great fortitude in the face of adversity. To account for this, the Bavarian player rolls a die at the start of the game. The indicated number of units of the Bavarian player's choice (which must be designated immediately, be they starting forces or reinforcements) are upgraded one morale class.

(5) *The River Saale.* This watercourse may only be crossed at bridges or fords.

(6) *Fords.* The demolished bridges were given running repairs by the assaulting Prussians. They are best treated as fords. The following rules apply to these:

    (a) only Infantry or Skirmishers may use a ford.

    (b) It takes a complete turn to cross the River Saale via a ford.

    (c) Units may not fire on the turn during which they use a ford.

(7) *The Nüdlinger Bach.* This insignificant obstacle is treated as a Stream.

(8) *Dense Woods.* Units may never enter wooded terrain, and are eliminated if forced to retreat into a wood.

Military Possibilities

(1) *Bavarian Demoralisation.* The initial Bavarian retreat is covered by the following rule. If the Prussians capture Kissingen, Hausen and Winkels before Turn 10, all Bavarian units immediately retreat one move and take a morale test. They are also all treated as being out of command.

(2) *Bavarian Blitzkrieg.* From Turn 10 onwards the Bavarian counter-attack begins. All units are treated as being in command for the remainder of the game: accordingly, the 'Royal Vacillation' special rule ceases to apply from the start of Turn 10.

(3) *Prussian Complacency.* General von Goeben's premature refitting exercise is covered by the following rule. If the Prussians capture Kissingen, Hausen, and Winkels before Turn 12, they must immediately act as follows:

(a) leave one unit garrisoning each captured town.

(b) withdraw all remaining units west of the River Saale via the bridge at Kissingen.

These restrictions are lifted at the start of Turn 12, from which point all Prussian units may act as desired.

(4) *Regal Resolution.* This rule allows players to explore what might have happened had Prince Carl displayed greater ability (or indeed if a more competent officer had led the Bavarian army). To account for this possibility, the 'Royal Vacillation' special rule no longer applies. Also, a further three Bavarian units (in addition to those covered by the 'Survival of the Fittest' rule) are upgraded one morale class.

(5) *Enlightened Artillery Doctrine.* This rule explores what might have happened if the Prussian artillery had acted with greater boldness. The following considerations apply:

(a) units 1, 3 and 12 are reclassified as 'Steel Rifled Artillery' (they are assumed to realise the potential of their new Krupp guns).

(b) the 'Save the Guns' special rule no longer applies.

(6) *Prussian Dragoons.* These horsemen (represented by unit 17) were trained to operate dismounted, although they invariably preferred to act as traditional mounted cavalry. Unit 17 may however be reclassified as Dragoons (equipped with Early Breechloading Rifles) if desired.

Victory Conditions

The Prussian player wins if he or she controls Kissingen, Winkels and Hausen at the end of Turn 15. Failure to do so results in a Bavarian victory.

Chapter 15

The Battle of Mars-La-Tour (16 August 1870)

HISTORICAL ACCOUNT

The events of the Seven Weeks War came as a spectacularly un-welcome surprise for France. Its Bonapartist regime had not expected such a rapid or decisive Prussian victory, and was unable to exploit the strategic potential provided by having two neighbouring great powers in a state of war. In particular, the failure to mobilise the French army at the start of the Austro-Prussian imbroglio was a grievous error: for if Napoleon III had taken this step, his forces could potentially have marched on the Rhineland. This threat would in turn have forced Prussia to commit additional forces to Western Germany, thereby weakening her main attack upon Austria, prolonging the war in the process. The French army need not, moreover, have had to attack – the mere threat to do so would have had the desired effect of rendering the Prussian assault less powerful. However, military expenditure was unpopular in France, and Napoleon III felt unable to take such a politically risky decision as mobilising his army.

This lost opportunity made the French even more desperate to achieve foreign policy success – this was deemed essential for a Bonapartist government which aspired to be the heir of Emperor Napoleon I. Another chance to make an impact soon arose over the future of Luxemburg. This piece of European real estate was currently administered by the Netherlands, who were finding the financial burden of doing so to be something of a strain. Accord-ingly, Napoleon III suggested that the French government purchase Luxemburg from the Dutch. The latter were keen to accept Napoleon III's offer: however, at this point a Prussian objection arose. For the latter state had a garrison deployed in Luxemburg, and German nationalists were appalled at the prospect of their troops making way for the French. The prospective deal was killed as a result.

The French Bonapartists were now exceptionally worried about achieving greater prestige, especially after domestic agitation had forced Napoleon III to concede a more liberal constitution: this would inevitably undermine imperial authority unless loyalty to the emperor could be buttressed by successes abroad. Accordingly, the French were determined to exploit the next diplomatic flash-point, which promptly occurred with one of the periodic crises over the succession to the Spanish throne. One of the few candidates prepared to accept what had become the political equivalent of a poisoned chalice was a member of the Prussian House of Hohenzollern: Prince Leopold von Hohenzollern-Sigmaringen. Leopold's cause was initially strong, but his chances were aborted thanks to delays on the part of the Spanish. However, the French wanted more than this *de facto* failure; they wanted a formal Prussian acknowledgement of non-interference in Spanish affairs. These demands were made at an informal meeting between the French Ambassador to Berlin, Count Vincente Benedetti, and the Prussian King Wilhelm, an encounter which occurred by chance at the spa resort of Bad Ems. The meeting was perfectly friendly, although it ended in disappointment for the French as Wilhelm explained that he was unable to accept any formal demands, and that further contact could only take place at an official governmental level. The Prussian King said as much in a telegram to his chief minister in Berlin, Otto von Bismarck.

The matter was not however to end there, for Bismarck was never one to let a diplomatic opportunity slip. Prussia's chief minister was especially aware of the potential instability created by the inde-pendent southern German states – and was especially determined that they became bound to Prussia, and never allied themselves to France. Accordingly, Bismarck decided to make political mischief out of the events at Bad Ems, by editing King Wilhelm's telegram, and releasing the contents to the Prussian press. This expurgated version of events made it look as if Benedetti had made impertinent demands upon King Wilhelm, who had responded by brusquely expelling the ambassador from the royal presence! Bismarck was fully aware that this would serve to inflame popular opinion both in Prussia and in France. His aim was to humiliate the French, thereby

156

weakening their position in Germany – and forcing the southern German states to ally themselves with Prussia. Bismarck was also entirely willing to go to war over the issue, for he was confident that the Prussian army would prevail over the French. War would also force the southern German states to take sides, and that meant fighting alongside the Prussians (their populations would never have allowed them to become allies of the French, even if their rulers had wanted to). Napoleon III was also ready to fight; he felt that yet another political humiliation would undermine his regime. France accordingly declared war on Prussia on 19 July 1870.

It has to be said that the French army was poorly equipped for the impending struggle. Its more enlightened officers were fully aware of just how much the army needed reform: it badly needed both numerical expansion, and an educated leadership. The desirability of a mass army was generally acknowledged; implementing the necessary measures was an altogether different matter. Tentative proposals were enacted in 1867, but more radical ideas of general conscription foundered on three difficulties. The first of these was political: the French population feared that a mass army would allow Napoleon III to implement a military dictatorship. Secondly, many men were conspicuously unwilling to serve as conscripts; and whereas this was understandable for true liberals, it must be said that all too many nationalists were only willing to embrace the concept of military glory, so long as others did the fighting for them – a thought process that was both logically inconsistent and morally dubious. Finally, the victories in the Crimea, Italy and in the colonial theatre of Algeria, seemed to prove the superiority of French arms (the embarrassing failure in Mexico, where the French support of Emperor Maximillian ended in humiliating defeat, was conveniently forgotten).

Entrenched military conservatism did not simply prevent the introduction of a mass army, but also served to retard the development of an educated officer corps. For the successes in Algeria and Italy had led to a belief in the efficacy of leadership by example: education was frowned upon, when contrasted with personal bravery. The apotheosis of this concept was embodied in the person of Marshal Achille Bazaine who, having failed his officer entrance examination, entered the army as a private but succeeded in reaching the highest rank, thanks to a thoroughly merited reputation for personal bravery. Events were to prove that courage on its own was not enough in 1870.

French success was dependent both upon speedy mobilisation and a rapid offensive, so that the Prussians could be defeated before they were at full strength. Unfortunately for the French, their rail network did not allow for the rapid embodiment of all their potential manpower: it took a long time for all the reserves and recruits to become ready for combat. In the meantime, three armies were formed. The Army of Alsace under Marshal MacMahon (an aristocratic officer of Irish descent) was based at Strasbourg; the Army of Lorraine under Marshal Bazaine was located at the fortress of Metz; and the Army of Châlons was busy collecting reserves and recruits at its titular base.

Both Bazaine and MacMahon marched towards Germany, hoping that their men would prove themselves in battle – much in particular was expected of the infantry, whose new Chassepot infantry rifle was to prove itself vastly superior to the Prussian Dreyse needle gun. The same could not unfortunately be said of the French artillery, whose ordnance was woefully inferior to the Krupp rifled guns which now equipped the Prussian army, following the lessons learned from the poor performance of the latter's artillery in 1866. The biggest French problem was however at the grand tactical and strategic level: the Bonapartist commanders proved themselves unable to concentrate enough men at the decisive point. This was in complete contrast to the Prussians, whose rapid mobilisation and comprehensive railway network, allowed them to meet the French challenge. Thus it was that MacMahon's offensive found itself checked by defeats at the Battles of Wissembourg (4th August) and Wörth (6th August); Bazaine was also defeated on the same day as the latter engagement, at the Battle of Spicheren.

The triple failure at these battles resulted in Napoleon III ordering a general retreat, which saw MacMahon fall back on Châlons, whilst Bazaine retired to Metz. This placed the French in a very difficult position, for Metz was far to the east of Châlons – and if Bazaine allowed his entire army to be besieged in the fortress, both French imperial armies would be surrounded, and could be defeated in detail.

It has to be said that the Prussians were unaware of the full extent of their opportunities. This was principally because neither antagonist used its cavalry effectively; horsemen were all too frequently retained for battlefield action, and not deployed in a scouting role as they should have been. As a result, Bazaine was presented with a priceless opportunity on 16th August, for the Prussian forces in the area of Mars-La-Tour, west of Metz, were pitifully weak. Bazaine's Army of Metz (as the Army of Lorraine had been re-named following its retreat) could have burst through the Prussian units and joined with MacMahon at Châlons. The combined army would undoubtedly have been in a position to confront the Prussians – especially as French recruits were gathering in increasing numbers, and their foes were necessarily operating in hostile territory.

Marshal Bazaine had 130,000 men under his command at Mars-La-Tour. His opponent, General Konstantin von Alvensleben, started the day with just 30,000 (reinforcements would increase that total to 65,000 by the end of the battle). The Prussian commander originally thought that the bulk of Bazaine's army had already retreated, having rather rashly assumed that the French would act as promptly as the Prussians would have done had the situation been reversed. Alvensleben consequently believed that he could isolate and destroy what he thought was Bazaine's rearguard.

The battle began when General von Alvensleben ordered his 5th infantry division to attack the village of Rézonville, only for the assaulting units to collide with an entire French infantry corps. The Prussians now had to revert to a defensive posture, at around 11.00am (the situation at this point is when the wargame starts; unit deployment is illustrated on the map provided). Alvensleben remained steady, however; he relied upon his artillery to stabilise the situation, and the shells that rained upon the French infantry brought them to a halt. Among the first casualties of the Prussian artillery was Colonel Ardant du Picq, the noted military theorist whose works were cited in Chapter 1.

Marshal Bazaine had a great opportunity to outflank the Prussian lines and take Mars-La-Tour, thereby opening up an escape route westwards. Unfortunately, Bazaine was utterly incapable of giving any orders, and was entirely unaware of what was going on, being more concerned with defending rather than attacking Alvensleben's relatively puny army. Nor were Bazaine's subordinates any better: they were obsessed with protecting their own flanks, rather than undergoing any added risks by seizing the initiative.

The French numbers were still having an effect, however, despite the truly execrable leadership at all levels. The Prussians were taking serious casualties by 2.00pm, so much so that Alvensleben ordered General von Friedrich Wilhelm von Bredow's cavalry brigade (unit 'J' in the wargame) forward to charge the enemy. Bredow was fully aware that cavalry charges were suicide missions in 1870, but still led his men forward (albeit after delaying as long as was politic). Fortunately for the Prussian horsemen, their commander was a skilled tactician who knew exactly what he was doing. Von Bredow made clever use of undulating terrain and battlefield smoke to conceal his approach as long as possible: as a result, he was able to launch a successful charge against all the odds. Bredow's brigade still lost 420 men out of 800 (Otto von Bismarck's son Herbert was among the wounded); but his charge managed to disorder and demoralise Marshal François-Antoine Canrobert's 6th French corps.

Bredow's charge may have stabilised the situation, but the Prussian position was still perilous, since additional French corps under Marshals Ladmirault and Leboeuf arrived at Bruville from 3.00pm. Their attacks were however not prosecuted with any more vigour than that displayed by the rest of the army, owing to the utter lack of any strategic direction. That was the job of Marshal Bazaine, but the latter was still obsessed with protecting his base, and seemed to be constitutionally incapable of launching any attack. It should not be assumed that Bazaine's physical courage was in question; he issued orders to individual regiments and led them personally on occasion. The sad fact was that personal bravery and moral steadiness were not always synonymous: Marshal Bazaine showed that a courageous commander was not necessarily a good general; his failure showed just how deficient was the French army's stress upon valour rather than intellect.

As a consequence of French dithering, elements of the Prussian 10th Corps under General Konstantin von Voights-Rhetz, arrived in time to plug the gap in the line. Faced with this new barrier, the French refused to attack. A final clash of cavalry units in the area of Mars-La-Tour was the last act in the battle, which concluded after a loss of around 16,000 men on each side. Bazaine ordered a retreat on the village of Gravelotte (just east of entry point 'B' on the map).

The French had now definitively lost their chance to break through – although some would argue that Bazaine botched another chance two days later at the Battle of Gravelotte – St Privat, where despite inflicting more losses than he received, he ordered a retreat upon Metz. It would now be up to MacMahon's army to relieve Bazaine; his efforts to do so will be covered in the next chapter.

THE WARGAME
Game Duration
The game lasts a total of 15 turns. The French go first in each turn.

Wargame Forces: The French Army
Marshal Bazaine's initial forces are deployed on the map as indicated, and are classified as follows:

Unit Type	Map Designation
Skirmishers (Elite, Later Breechloading Rifle)	1, 8
Line Infantry (Average, Later Breechloading Rifle, Loose Order)	2, 3, 5, 7
Artillery (Smoothbore)	4, 6
Cavalry (Average)	9
Imperial Guard Infantry (Elite, Later Breechloading Rifle, Loose Order)	10, 11

Mars-La-Tour was a large scale battle. Readers should consider my remarks in Chapter 6, and bear in mind that I am creating a general representation of the battlefield situation, rather than a precise replication of the numbers involved (that would require a vast number of figures). This scenario demonstrates the numerical advantage of the French army compared with its opponent, but deliberately enfeebles the Gallic effort by imposing rigid leadership restrictions, thereby accounting for Bazaine's indecision (a military possibility covers what might have happened if the French commander had been wounded or killed during one of his visits to the front line). French success in this battle will depend largely upon the wargamer's ability to deploy enough Infantry units in a position where the Chassepot rifle can have a measurable effect upon the enemy.

Several French units enter as reinforcements, the schedule for which is indicated below:

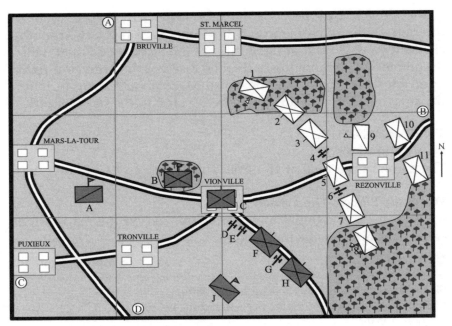

Map 11. The Battle of Mars-La-Tour

Turn of Arrival	Unit Type	Unit Designation	Entry Point
7	Line Infantry (Average, Later Breechloading Rifle, Loose Order)	12, 13	A
7	Skirmishers (Elite, Later Breechloading Rifle)	14	A
7	Artillery (Smoothbore)	15	A
9	Line Infantry (Average, Later Breechloading Rifle, Loose Order)	16, 17	A
9	Cavalry (Average)	18, 19	A

Wargame Forces: The Prussian Army

General von Alvensleben's initial forces are deployed on the map as indicated and are classified as follows:

Unit Type	Map Designation
Cavalry (Average)	A
Skirmishers (Fanatic, Early Breechloading Rifle)	B
Infantry (Elite, Early Breechloading Rifle, Loose Order)	C, F, H

Artillery (Steel Rifled)	D, E, G
Bredow's Cavalry (Fanatic)	J

The numerical inferiority of the Prussian army is reflected in the wargame, with the significant exception of the Prussian Artillery. Alvensleben deployed his ordnance with great skill during the battle, so that its existing technical superiority over its French counterpart was magnified even farther. This can only be reflected by giving the Prussian army more artillery units than the French; the latter may have had more guns, but proved themselves incapable of deploying or using them with any effectiveness.

The remarkable deeds of Bredow's cavalrymen must also be depicted in the wargame. In terms of strict scale, Bredow's troopers only formed a part of unit 'J'; however, their effectiveness can only be displayed by conflating their numbers to form an entire wargames unit. A special rule also allows for the disproportionate moral effect of Bredow's charge upon its unfortunate victims.

A small number of Prussian units enter the game as reinforcements, the schedule for which is indicated below:

Turn of Arrival	Unit Type	Unit Designation	Entry Point
7	Infantry (Elite, Early Breechloading Rifle, Loose Order)	K	D
10	Infantry (Elite, Early Breechloading Rifle, Loose Order)	L	C
10	Cavalry (Average)	M	C

Special Rules

(1) *French Indecision.* The irresolute French leadership at the battle is covered by only allowing a portion of the army to move and fight with full effectiveness in each turn. The following procedure applies:

(a) the French player rolls a die at the start of each of his or her turns, in order to determine how many units are in command:

Die Roll	Units in Command
1–2	1
3–4	2
5–6	3

163

(b) the French chooses which units he or she wishes to place In Command. These units may act without any restrictions.

(c) units that are Out of Command may not declare charges. They also only move at half their normal speed, and roll half the usual number of dice when firing during their own turn (defensive fire against enemy charges is not affected).

(2) *Metz Obsession.* Marshal Bazaine's extreme concerns over protecting his base are reflected by mandating that any French unit starting its turn west of Vionville or St Marcel is always Out of Command.

(3) *Mitrailleuse.* This primitive machine gun was deployed with French Artillery units. Its effects are depicted by allowing French Artillery to roll an extra die when engaging targets at short range (up to 12cm).

(4) *Bazaine Visits The Front.* To account for Bazaine's temporary leadership of frontline units, the French player rolls a die at the start of each Prussian turn. On a roll of 5–6, the French automatically pass the first morale test they are mandated to take as the result of enemy firing during the Prussian turn.

(5) *French Refit.* To reflect the overwhelming French numbers, they are allowed to take reinforcements from their eliminated bases once in the game. This is done by collecting all eliminated bases and forming new units from them (for example, if 10 Infantry bases have been eliminated, they may form 2 complete units of 4 bases each, and one unit with 2 bases). The following restrictions apply on the turn during which the French Refit rule applies:

(a) no French units may move or fire.

(b) the reconstituted units enter the game at entry point 'B' at the start of the following French turn.

(6) *Death Riders.* The spectacular effects of Bredow's charge (which became known as the 'Death Ride') are covered by the following rules:

(a) whenever Bredow's Cavalry (unit J) declares a charge for the first time during the game, its target must take 4 morale tests the instant it is engaged in hand-to-hand combat.

(b) if Bredow's Cavalry wins its first hand-to-hand combat, all French units within 20cm must each take 2 morale tests.

Military Possibilities

(1) *Bazaine Takes A Bullet.* The possibility of Marshal Bazaine becoming killed or wounded during one of his visits to the frontline, and being replaced by a more dynamic commander, is covered by the following rules:

    (a) the French player rolls a die at the start of his or her turn. On a roll of 6, Bazaine becomes a casualty. No French units may move or fire on the turn during which Bazaine is rendered a casualty.

    (b) from the next turn onwards, the number of French units In Command is doubled (see the Special Rule covering 'French Indecision').

    (c) the 'Metz Obsession' rule no longer applies.

(2) *Infantry Support.* This rule covers what might have happened if the French had deployed their Mitrailleuse machine guns with Infantry, rather than Artillery units. This unlikely possibility is covered by the following rules:

    (a) the 'Mitrailleuse' Special Rule no longer applies.

    (b) the French player selects 2 Infantry units at the start of the game. These are assumed to have been supplied with Mitrailleuse machine guns, the effects of which are simulated by allowing both nominated units to re-roll any dice that register a miss when firing.

(3) *French Artillery.* The French ordnance was actually rifled, but underperformed rather badly owing to technical problems, which is why it is classified as 'Smoothbore'. To evaluate what might have happened if the difficulties had been dealt with, French Artillery can be reclassified as 'Bronze Rifled'.

Victory Conditions

The French player wins if there are no Prussian units within 20cm of the road running between Mars-La-Tour and Entry Point 'B', at the end of Turn 15. Failure to achieve this condition results in a Prussian victory.

Chapter 16

The Battle of Sedan (1 September 1870)

HISTORICAL ACCOUNT

It has often been said that the German nation has a great organisational efficiency. This supposedly racial trait owes its genesis to observations of Prussian military activity during the second half of the nineteenth century: General von Moltke realised that victory in battle did not go purely to the big battalions, but to those which operated with the greatest efficiency – which in turn required organisational and logistical excellence. These factors were displayed in abundance the day after the Battle of Gravelotte, when Moltke reorganised his armies in order to exploit new opportunities. Thus it was that the Prussian 1st Army besieged Metz along with part of the 2nd Army (Moltke also used this as an opportunity to dismiss the consistently impetuous and insubordinate General Karl von Steinmetz, the erstwhile commander of 1st Army). The rest of 2nd Army combined with miscellaneous troops to form the newly created Army of the Meuse, which promptly headed towards Châlons along with 3rd Army. This complex piece of reorganisation was moreover carried out within a single day; absolutely no momentum was lost, and the sole result was that the Prussian armies operated with even greater efficiency.

The same could not be said for the French forces, whose combined leadership continued to display chronic indecision and inefficiency. Marshal Patrice MacMahon, the commander of the Army of Châlons, had the unenviable task of trying to regain the initiative from the Prussians. MacMahon had three options: he could stand and fight at Châlons, in the hope that enough recruits would join his forces in time to confront the Prussians; he could withdraw westwards to Paris, collecting additional recruits and drawing the

Prussians further away from their supply base in the process; or he could attempt to relieve Metz, which would entail leaving Châlons and Paris unguarded whilst MacMahon's forces moved northwards and then eastwards around the Prussian flanks, reaching Bazaine's Metz garrison in the process.

The obvious military decision was to order a withdrawal to Paris. This would not only allow MacMahon enough time to gather substantial numbers of new recruits, but could also allow Marshal Bazaine to launch aggressive sorties in the process – thereby weakening those invading forces devoted to attacking the Army of Châlons. Unfortunately for the French, the militarily sensible plan was a political impossibility: the Imperial régime had already lost so much credibility that another retreat might lead to its being overthrown by a popular rebellion. These political considerations also ruled out simply standing and fighting at Châlons, since the public demanded aggressive intent. As a result, the only option was to relieve Metz. This would certainly achieve every conceivable political goal: for the Army of Châlons was to be accompanied by Napoleon III in person, and the spectacle of Bazaine being relieved by the Emperor marching at the head of his troops, would have killed any political opposition stone dead.

The chosen option of relieving Metz would certainly have needed true Napoleonic flair if it was to succeed. For its chosen instrument, the Army of Châlons, was badly shaken by its defeats at Wissembourg and Wörth, and was moreover just half the size of its Prussian enemies – a situation that would only change after Metz could be relieved. As if this was not enough to cope with, the proposed march around the Prussian flanks would necessarily present the Army of Châlons' own flank to the enemy army.

The French plan nevertheless started well, with their initial march northwards being undetected by the Prussians. General von Moltke was accordingly astonished when his forces arrived at Châlons on 24 August only to find the city unoccupied. The Prussians did however soon adapt to this unforeseen situation; cavalry patrols ranged far and wide in an attempt to locate the French. Moltke was also greatly assisted by the uncensored Parisian press which dutifully if irresponsibly reported each and every rumour it heard – and duly informed the Prussians of MacMahon's real objective in the process!

Thanks largely to the assistance they received from French journalists, the Prussians were able to detect MacMahon's forces fairly rapidly. Moltke responded promptly, and ordered his armies forward: he wanted to see the Army of Châlons surrounded and wiped out. The Prussians were greatly assisted in their endeavours by Marshal Bazaine, whose by now customary inactivity meant that the fortress of Metz remained largely quiet and only required a relatively small force of Prussian besiegers as a result.

By 30 August, the Army of Châlons was on the receiving end of Moltke's offensive, for that day saw MacMahon's 5th Corps soundly defeated at the Battle of Beaumont. The French fell back to Sedan as a result, where they found themselves pursued by the vengeful Prussians. Sedan itself had few supplies available; there was no time to rest and refit in any case. The only hope for the French was that they broke away to the northwest, before Sedan was encircled by Moltke's forces. Unfortunately for the Imperial cause, MacMahon spent 31st August dithering, and by the following day it was too late: 230,000 Prussian troops had encircled 120,000 French.

The Prussian forces relied largely upon their superior artillery to bombard the French lines: they had no desire to expose their troops to the deadly Chassepot rifle any more than was absolutely essential. (The deployment of the respective armies is indicated on the sketch map for the wargame; readers should note that the Prussian forces west of the River Meuse are not depicted, since they simply contained the French within Sedan and did not play any part in engaging the main portion of the Army of Châlons.) The Prussian ordnance soon took effect, with Marshal MacMahon being wounded early in the battle. This inevitably brought about a leadership crisis in the French ranks, with much confusion and squabbling ensuing over precisely who should take charge. Command eventually passed to General Immanuel Wimpffen, much to the displeasure of General Auguste-Alexandre Ducros, who also wanted the job. Not that it would have made much difference whoever had been in charge, for the French position was hopeless. Thus it was that the villages of Floing, Illy, and Givonne fell to the Prussians, while Balan was taken by their Bavarian allies.

By 1.00pm the French situation was desperate. Their sole remaining hope lay in breaking through the Prussian lines between Floing and Illy, thereby securing a retreat to the northwest. However, the only reserves available were cavalry units. These behaved with conspicuous gallantry, but had no chance of prevailing against a fully prepared defence, and were soon wiped out. This calamity represented a far more telling guide to the future of horsemen on the battlefield than von Bredow's success at Mars-La-Tour, although the cavalrymen themselves were unwilling to entertain the mere possibility of the traditional charge becoming militarily redundant.

The battle continued until late evening, but the French were utterly without hope. The entire army surrendered the following day, along with Napoleon III, who had behaved bravely during the battle despite his ill-health. The Emperor refused to abdicate, hoping to continue ruling his country. However, his cause was doomed as only Bazaine's Metz garrison remained undefeated (it surrendered to the Prussians on 28 October). On 4 September, the Napoleonic régime was overthrown, and replaced by the Third Republic, which resolved to continue the struggle.

The Republican phase of the war relied upon the deployment of popular armies, whose ranks were bolstered by enthusiastic if not always highly trained or well equipped volunteers. Their consistent aim was to relieve the Prussian siege of Paris. Their very existence appalled the Germanic armies. For the Prussian military code believed in regular, disciplined forces waging war according to specific rules: the advent of popular warfare seemed both disorderly and bestial. The fact that the Republicans often displayed greater spirit and better leadership than their Imperial predecessors doubt-less proved even more unwelcome to their foes. However, the Prussians still had more than enough ability to prevail, and a general agreement was reached on 26 February 1871. This culmin-ated in the Treaty of Frankfurt, signed on 10 May, by whose terms the French paid an indemnity of 5 billion francs, and ceded the provinces of Alsace and Lorraine to Germany.

It was especially noteworthy that the two border provinces were given to Germany, not to Prussia. For the German Empire was created on 18 January 1871 in the Hall of Mirrors at Versailles, when King Wilhelm of Prussia was crowned Emperor Wilhelm of Germany. Otto von Bismarck's aim was achieved: nationalism had been controlled and tamed, becoming the servant of Prussian authoritarianism rather than a threat to it – for the new régime was utterly dominated by Prussian values and social structures.

However, the insistence upon territorial acquisitions served only to arouse resentment among the French people, and promoted a desire for revenge rather than resigned acceptance. All this showed the dangers of popular passions in international affairs: the Vienna settlement of 1815 had by contrast been created in a different age, where moderation was held to promote stability, and largely did so. The dismal consequences of impassioned nationalism only promoted tension and conflict, whose dreadful results were seen with the outbreak of the First World War in 1914.

THE WARGAME
Game Duration
The game lasts a total of 15 turns. The Prussians go first in each turn.

Wargame Forces: The Prussian Army
General von Moltke's entire army starts the game on the table as indicated on the map provided. Its units are classified as follows:

Unit Type	Map Designation
Prussian Skirmishers (Fanatic, Early Breechloading Rifle)	1, 9
Prussian Infantry (Elite, Early Breechloading Rifle, Loose Order)	2, 6, 7, 10, 15, 16
Prussian Artillery (Steel Rifled)	3, 4, 5, 12, 13, 14
Prussian Cavalry (Average)	8, 11
Bavarian Skirmishers (Elite, Rifled Musket)	17
Bavarian Cavalry (Average)	18
Bavarian Infantry (Average, Rifled Musket, Loose Order)	19, 23, 24
Bavarian Artillery (Steel Rifled)	20, 21, 22

The power of the Prussian Artillery is reflected by the large number of units fielded; the ordnance played a vital role during the historical battle, and must therefore do so in any wargame which depicts the engagement. The overwhelming numbers and extremely competent organisation of the Prussian army (from which its Bavarian allies benefited greatly) are also reflected in the special rule covering refitting: it will be noted that this causes no disruption to normal military activity (unlike the equivalent rule covering the shambolic French effort at Mars-La-Tour).

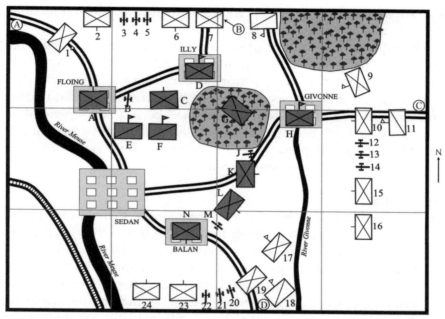

Map 12. The Battle of Sedan

Wargame Forces: The French Army

Marshal MacMahon's army starts the game as illustrated on the map. Its units are classified as follows:

Unit Type	Map Designation
Infantry (Average, Later Breechloading Rifle, Loose Order)	A, C, G, K, L, N
Artillery (Smoothbore)	B, J, M
Skirmishers (Elite, Later Breechloading Rifle)	D, H
Cavalry (Average)	E, F

The French are badly outnumbered in their wargame, and have very little chance of winning. Their only hope of doing so will occur if enough units escape via entry point 'A', which event is unlikely to happen without inept Prussian play. It is possible that the French can hang on for a nominal draw (this is a reward for doing rather better than MacMahon and his fellow generals did in the real battle), but their chances are not high; this wargame is designed to show

171

the appalling situation the French got themselves in, rather than provide a balanced encounter.

The military possibilities provide some scope for exploring what could have happened if Bazaine and MacMahon had been decidedly more competent than their historical performance. They will provide for interesting games, but it must be remembered that neither contingency was likely: for if Bazaine had been a better general he would never have been besieged in Metz in the first place; and if MacMahon had displayed greater initiative, he would not have allowed his army to become surrounded at all.

Special Rules

(1) *Prussian Refit*. To reflect the overwhelming Prussian numbers, they are allowed to take reinforcements from eliminated bases as often as they wish, at the start of any turn. This is done by collecting eliminated bases and forming as many units as desired (for example, if seven Infantry bases have been eliminated, the Prussian player has two options. He or she may create two units, one of 4 bases and one with 3 bases; alternatively, a single unit of 4 bases may be formed, with the remaining 3 bases left in the eliminated pile, to be used to create a new unit on a subsequent turn). Refitting Prussian units may enter the game from entry points 'B' or 'C'; Bavarian units enter the table from entry point 'D'.

(2) *River Givonne*. This is treated as a stream.

(3) *River Meuse*. This is a river, and may not be crossed at any point.

(4) *Sedan*. No unit may enter Sedan at any time. Any unit forced to do so by a retreat is eliminated (this is because any forces in Sedan were devoted to covering the Prussian units west of the River Meuse, which do not need to be depicted on the table).

(5) *Mitrailleuse*. This primitive machine gun was deployed with French Artillery units. Its effects are depicted by allowing French Artillery to roll an extra die when engaging targets at short range (up to 12cm).

Military Possibilities

(1) *Bazaine Attacks*. Marshal Bazaine is assumed to launch a concerted sortie from Metz. If this rule is used, then the 'Prussian

Refit' rule no longer applies; the reinforcements are instead devoted to containing Bazaine.

(2) *French Urgency.* Marshal MacMahon is assumed to have been fully aware of his army's impending doom, and to have ordered an attempt to breakout from Sedan on 31 August. To investigate this possibility, units 5, 7, 9, 11, 14 and 16 are removed from the Prussian order of battle, and play no part in the wargame.

(3) *Infantry Support.* The unlikely possibility of the French transferring the Mitrailleuse machine gun from Artillery to Infantry units, is covered by the following provisions:

(a) the 'Mitrailleuse' special rule no longer applies.

(b) the French player selects 3 Infantry units at the start of the game. These are assumed to have been equipped with the Mitrailleuse, the effects of which are simulated by allowing all 3 nominated units to re-roll any dice that register a miss when firing.

(4) *French Artillery.* As already stated in the Mars-La-Tour scenario, the French artillery was rifled, but is graded as 'Smoothbore' to reflect its poor technical performance. To see what might have happened if these limitations had been addressed in time, the French Artillery can be reclassified as 'Bronze Rifled' if desired.

Victory Conditions

(1) *French Victory.* The French player wins the game by exiting 4 units from the table via entry point 'A'. Units that exit the map may never return.

(2) *Prussian Victory.* If the French player fails to achieve his or her victory conditions, then the Prussian player can win the game by occupying Floing, Illy, Givonne and Balan at the end of Turn 15.

(3) *Draw.* If neither player fulfils their victory conditions, the game is drawn.

Appendix 1

Bibliography

I have listed all the works I found especially useful when writing this book, and have appended brief comments to each entry in order to give prospective readers an idea of each volume's content and likely utility.

Some of the books listed are no longer in print. They can be found in local libraries, or through the military book suppliers listed in Appendix 3.

WARGAMES BOOKS

Asquith, Stuart, *The Partizan Press Guide to Solo Wargaming* (Partizan Press, 2006). A solo wargame is a game in which the actions of one side are determined according to a set of options that are often generated randomly. This book is an outstanding introduction to the subject.

Featherstone, Donald, *Advanced War Games* (Stanley Paul, 1969). A compilation of many stimulating rules design concepts.

Featherstone, Donald, *War Games Campaigns* (Stanley Paul, 1970). Many wargamers dream of fighting complete campaigns, rather than confining themselves to isolated battles. This groundbreaking work represents the classic introduction to its subject. It includes four chapters devoted specifically to nineteenth-century Europe.

Featherstone, Donald, *War Games through the Ages, Volume Three: 1792–1859* (Stanley Paul, 1975), and *War Games through the Ages, Volume Four: 1861–1945* (Stanley Paul, 1976). These books were intended to provide historical background for wargamers, which they do extremely well. They also contain some useful ideas on how to simulate the periods on the wargames table.

Featherstone, Donald, *Battles with Model Soldiers* (David and Charles, 1984). The wonderfully simple ruleset in this introductory book

174

can easily be adapted for wargames set in nineteenth-century Europe.

Featherstone, Donald, *Solo Wargaming* (John Curry, 2009; originally 1973). The first book published on its subject, packed full of fascinating ideas.

Featherstone, Donald, *Lost Tales* (John Curry, 2009). A collection of new and old material, including the set of late-nineteenth century wargames rules first published in the legendary but now defunct *Wargamer's Newsletter* magazine.

Grant, Charles Stewart, *Scenarios for Wargames* (Wargames Research Group, 1981). This especially useful book contains a huge variety of fascinating wargaming encounters that deliver intriguing games.

Grant, Charles Stewart, *Programmed Wargames Scenarios* (Wargames Research Group, 1983). Similar to the previous work, but intended for the solo wargamer.

Grant, C.S., *Wargame Campaigns* (CSG Publications, 1985). A fine contribution to the genre pioneered by Donald Featherstone.

Grant, C.S. and Asquith, S.A. *Scenarios For All Ages* (CSG Publications, 1996). Another book of challenging wargames encounters.

Gush, George and Finch, Andrew, *A Guide to Wargaming* (Croom Helm, 1980). This book is especially valuable for its analysis of wargames design theory. It also contains a good set of rules devoted to the later nineteenth century.

Reisswitz, B. von, *Kriegsspiel* (Too Fat Lardies, 2007; originally 1824). The first set of wargames rules ever designed is now available in this publication. The rather dense and turgid prose style makes for a complex ruleset, but it does represent an essential and highly influential part of the history of wargaming.

Verdy du Vernois, Julius A.F.W. von, *Free Kriegspiel* (John Curry, 2008; originally 1876). The bulk of this book consists of a battle report of a 'free *kriegspiel*' wargame: as such, it forms another vital part of wargaming history (leaden prose notwithstanding). The book also contains the rules for the British Army's 'free *kriegspiel*' wargame of 1896 – players inspired to create a simulation of this type can use these rules as an indispensable source.

Weigle, Bruce, *1870* (Medieval Miscellanea, 2001), *1859* (Medieval Miscellanea, 2006) and *1866* (Medieval Miscellanea, 2010). These volumes contain workmanlike sets of wargames rules. They are however most valuable for the historical analysis therein; the outstanding sets of scenarios, including some superb maps of historical battlefields; and the massively detailed annotated bibliographies. The first volume covers the Franco-Prussian War; the second examines the Franco-Austrian and Second Schleswig Wars; and the third analyses the Seven Weeks War. The quality of the scholarship and fluency of the prose make all three books essential for the dedicated wargamer.

Wells, H.G., *Little Wars* (Arms and Armour Press, 1970: originally 1913). This marvellous book popularised wargaming. It comprises a beautifully written encapsulation of the joy to be obtained from the hobby – its charm is enhanced by J.R. Sinclair's wonderful marginal illustrations. Wells' rules are often frowned upon by self-styled apostles of realism, but provide for magnificently entertaining games – those who prefer a little more detail could derive much profit from consulting the book's Appendix on *kriegspiel*.

Wesencraft, C.F., *Practical Wargaming* (Elmfield Press, 1974). This classic work was years ahead of its time, and is finally beginning to receive the recognition it deserves. It contains many innovative ideas, from which I have derived a great deal of inspiration. Among the rulesets included is one devoted to the Franco-Prussian War.

MILITARY HISTORY

Ascoli, David, *A Day of Battle: Mars-La-Tour 16th August 1870* (Birlinn, 2001; originally 1987). The classic account of its subject. The book also includes much valuable detail on the Franco-Prussian War up to and including Napoleon III's surrender.

Badsey, Stephen, *The Franco-Prussian War 1870–1871* (Osprey, 2003) The Osprey Essential Histories are intended to provide accessible introductions to their subjects. This entry in the series fulfils its remit exceptionally well.

Barry, Quintin, *The Franco-Prussian War 1870–71, Volume 1: The Campaign of Sedan* (Helion, 2007) and *The Franco-Prussian War 1870–71, Volume 2: After Sedan* (Helion, 2007). These exceptionally detailed military histories are notable for the huge number of illustrations provided, including contemporary maps. The second volume is especially valuable, covering as it does the frequently neglected Republican phase of the war.

Barry, Quintin, *The Road to Königgrätz* (Helion, 2010). Another minutely detailed and impressively scholarly account, this one devoted to all aspects of the Seven Weeks War – the campaigns in Western Germany and Italy are not neglected.

Bavarian General Staff, *The Contribution of the Royal Bavarian Army to the War of 1866* (Helion, 2010; originally 1868). This book has all the virtues of an official military history, namely vast amounts of detail on its chosen subject – including orders of battle, actual strengths at various battles, and even casualty lists. It also possesses all the vices of its genre, chief among which are its occasionally leaden prose, and especially an unwillingness to criticise Prince Carl's somewhat singular leadership. It still represents essential reading for anyone interested in the Seven Weeks War in Western Germany.

Brett, Edward M., *The British Auxiliary Legion in the First Carlist War 1835–1838* (Four Courts Press, 2005). An entertaining and enlightening account of a largely forgotten subject.

Brooks, Richard, *The Battle of Froeschwiller 6th August 1870* (Continental Wars Society, 2006). This concise account of the battle (also referred to as the Battle of Wörth) provides an ideal guide for wargamers.

Brooks, Richard, *Solferino 1859* (Osprey, 2009). The Osprey Campaign series of titles aim to provide comprehensive yet concise accounts of their subjects – along with some fine illustrations in colour. This is a particularly fine example, providing as it does an account not only of Solferino, but of the Franco-Austrian War as a whole.

Cairns, Conrad, *The First Carlist War 1833–1840* (Perry Miniatures, 2009). This book has everything any wargamer could desire. It provides a fine history of the war, enlightening accounts of significant battles from the conflict, and some exquisite colour illustrations, especially of army uniforms.

Carpino, F. Brancaccio di, *The Fight for Freedom: Palermo, 1860* (Folio Society, 1968; originally 1900). This illuminating and entertaining eyewitness account provides a fine picture of the rotten Neapolitan regime, and the uprising against it.

Clausewitz, Carl von, *On War* (Princeton 1976; originally 1832). The first book to fully comprehend the nature of war in all its aspects. Many editions are available, including some at bargain prices.

Drury, Ian, *The Russo-Turkish War 1877* (Osprey, 1994). The Osprey Men-at-Arms titles are renowned for their provision of colour uniform illustrations. This work does a great deal more than that. It includes a brief account of the war, detail on the organisation of the respective armies, and information on their weaponry.

Ellis, John, *Cavalry: The History of Mounted Warfare* (Pen and Sword, 2004; originally 1978). This sound general history contains a passionate indictment of nineteenth-century European cavalry, ridiculing the continued belief in the efficacy of charge tactics against increasingly powerful weaponry.

Embree, Michael, *Bismarck's First War* (Helion, 2006). The only account of the Second Schleswig War currently available in English. The level of scholarship and detail is remarkable; both qualities are complemented by the vast number of illustrations, which include contemporary maps.

Ffrench Blake, R.L.V., *The Crimean War* (Pen and Sword 2006; originally 1971). A workmanlike and concise military history. The maps are particularly good.

Gates, David, *Warfare in the Nineteenth Century* (Palgrave, 2001). This solid introduction is strongest when exploring the strategic, political and cultural context of warfare.

Glover, Michael, *Warfare from Waterloo to Mons* (Book Club Associates, 1980). An outstandingly written introduction to warfare on land and sea, covering all the salient points extremely well.

Griffith, Paddy, *Forward into Battle* (Antony Bird, 1981). A fascinating account of battle tactics from Waterloo to Vietnam, noteworthy for its advocacy of the efficacy of shock tactics (increased firepower notwithstanding).

Griffith, Paddy, *Military thought in the French army, 1821–51* (Manchester University Press, 1989). This could have been a dry academic account of an obscure subject: the writer's erudition and literary flair ensure that it is not. There may be little detail on actual fighting, but there is a great deal of insight into how the army developed.

Harris, Henry, *The Alma 1854* (Charles Knight, 1971). The Knight's Battles for Wargamers series was renowned for its provision of battle histories in a concise format, with extensive maps. This book is a fine example.

Henderson, G.F.R., *The Battle of Spicheren: August 6th 1870* (Helion, 2009; originally 1891). The author was one of the most renowned military historians of his time. This account, intended for the education of Henderson's fellow British army officers, has won the reputation of being a military classic: its detail is immense and its analysis profound.

Hibbert, Christopher, *The Destruction of Lord Raglan* (Wordsworth 1999; originally 1961). A spirited attempt at defending the reputation of a much-maligned commander. This may be a controversial thesis: it is still an exceptionally well-written account that serves well as a history of the Crimean War.

Hold, Alexander, *History of the Campaign of 1866 in Italy* (Helion 2010; originally 1867). A thorough contemporary account of the Custoza campaign, written from an Austrian perspective.

Howard, Michael, *War in European History* (Oxford, 1976). This remarkable analysis of warfare from medieval to modern times not only outlines significant tactical developments, but puts military history into its socio-economic context. By any standards, this is an astonishing feat. The fact that the author can do so in just 150 pages makes it an incomparable one.

Howard, Michael, *The Franco-Prussian War* (Routledge 2002; originally 1961). This groundbreaking work has won classic status. Its erudition is remarkable; its judgements invariably considered; and its literary quality immense. Any student of the Franco-Prussian War should read this masterpiece.

McElwee, William, *The Art of War: Waterloo to Mons* (Weidenfeld and Nicholson 1974). A brilliant analytical survey of military developments during the nineteenth century.

Patry, Leonce, *The Reality of War* (Cassell, 2001: originally 1897) An illuminating memoir of the Franco-Prussian War, from the perspective of an astute French junior officer.

Pocock, John, *Bitter Victory* (Barbarossa, 2002). This treatment of the Custoza campaign in 1866 provides a perfect guide for any wargamer. It includes a fine historical account complete with maps, detailed uniform information (including some superb colour illustrations by Ralph Weaver), and some useful ideas on wargaming the campaign.

179

Pocock, John, *Langensalza 1866* (Continental Wars Society, 2002). Another excellent wargamer's guide from this publisher, containing a concise but perfectly judged account of this unjustifiably neglected battle between Hanover and Prussia. It includes uniform information, and advice on wargaming the battle.

Pocock, John, *The Royal Bavarian Army in the Campaign of 1866* (Continental Wars Society, 2003). Another fine wargamer's guide, along the lines of the author's preceding work on the Battle of Langensalza.

Russell, William Howard, *Despatches from the Crimea* (Frontline, 2008). The author was the most prominent of all the early war correspondents. His work on the Crimean War created a national storm: reading these despatches, it is easy to see why.

Sutherland, Stuart, *The Organization of the German State Forces in 1866* (Helion, 2010). This groundbreaking work details the organisation, numerical strength, and equipment of all German states (excluding Prussia) in 1866. It also contains detailed orders of battle for those forces which played an active part in the Seven Weeks War, as well as a useful chronology of the conflict. This book is likely to be of great interest for specialist readers; it is a truly monumental work of scholarship.

Svendsen, Nick, *The First Schleswig-Holstein War 1848–50* (Helion, 2008). This detailed military history is the only account of this war currently available in English.

Sweetman, John, *Balaclava 1854* (Osprey, 2005). An excellent entry in the Osprey Campaign series. This book includes a useful section on how to wargame the battle.

Unknown, *Roots of Strategy, Book 2* (Stackpole, 1987). The unnamed editor of this volume has done a truly splendid job in retrieving and reproducing edited editions of Ardant du Picq's *Battle Studies*, Jomini's *Art of War*, and Clausewitz's early work on the *Principles of War*. This book is essential reading for any student of military theory.

Viotti, Andrea, *Garibaldi: The Revolutionary and his Men* (Blandford, 1979). This book provides an entertaining celebration of its subjects and their achievements.

Wawro, Geoffrey, *The Austro-Prussian War* (Cambridge, 1996). This author has won a reputation for great literary flair and highly opinionated views. The latter trait may not be to the taste of pedants; more discerning readers will appreciate the quality provided when a writer not only has a myriad of ideas, but also possesses the ability to express them with real verve.

Wawro, Geoffrey, *The Franco-Prussian War* (Cambridge, 2003). Another outstanding military history which displays all the virtues displayed in the author's earlier work on the Seven Weeks War.

Weaver, Ralph, *Montebello 20 May 1859* (Continental Wars Society, 2003). This interesting concise work describes the battle through the medium of four eyewitness accounts.

GENERAL HISTORY

Cobban, Alfred, *A History of Modern France, Volume 2: 1799–1871* (Pelican, 1981: originally 1965) and *A History of Modern France, Volume 3: 1871–1962* (Pelican 1984; originally 1965). This very opinionated historian attracted the ire of his fellow academics for what they saw as his over-simplification of weighty issues. One suspects that this stemmed more from dislike of Cobban's healthy sales figures, as compared with their less startling literary achievements. These books actually contain a brilliant analysis of nineteenth-century France.

Craig, Gordon A., *The Politics of the Prussian Army 1640–1945* (Oxford, 1955). A classic examination of Prussian militarism and its political consequences, both toxic and benign.

Duggan, Christopher, *The Force of Destiny* (Allen Lane, 2007). This history of Italy since 1796 includes an especially informative examination of the growth of Italian nationalism.

Fraser, Rebecca, *A People's History of Britain* (Chatto and Windus, 2003). This beautifully written traditional history book is guaranteed to provide entertainment and enlightenment for all ages.

Kinross, Lord, *The Ottoman Centuries* (Morrow, 1977). A useful general introduction to the history of the Ottoman Empire, from its creation to its dissolution.

Kissinger, Henry, *A World Restored: Metternich, Castlereagh and the Problems of Peace 1812–1822* (Phoenix 2000; originally 1957). The author was to become one of the most controversial and divisive

American Secretaries of State in the twentieth century. This work dates from his period as a lecturer at Harvard. It provides a solid academic analysis of peacemaking, and is especially informative when examining conservative statecraft.

Marx, Karl and Engels, Frederick, *Selected Works* (Lawrence and Wishart, 1968). This outstanding selection of works provides an ideal grounding in all aspects of Marxist thought. The Communist Manifesto is included, as are Marx's historical polemics on Napoleon III's *coup d'état*, and the Paris Commune of 1871.

Mosse, George L., *The Culture of Western Europe* (Westview, 1988). A classic academic examination of the ideas that shaped a continent. This book is a vital source for anyone interested in the history of European thought.

Ozment, Steven, *A Mighty Fortress: A New History of the German People* (Granta, 2004). This work is a model of concision. Its examination of the German cultural and national identity is especially strong.

Seton-Watson, Hugh, *The Russian Empire 1901–1917* (Oxford, 1967). An outstandingly comprehensive work of scholarship, providing all the information anyone could ever require about its subject.

Taylor, A.J.P., *The Struggle for Mastery in Europe 1848–1918* (Oxford 1983; originally 1954). One of the best diplomatic histories ever written. The author's scholarly rigour is matched only by his literary flair: the two qualities combined to produce this masterpiece.

Taylor, A.J.P., *The Course of German History* (Methuen 1985; originally 1945). The author became known as 'the people's historian' during his lifetime, chiefly for the brilliance of his writing and the controversial nature of his opinions. Both traits came to the fore in this work, which argues that German political activity always had a predilection for authoritarianism, which culminated in its support for Adolf Hitler. Whatever the merit of such opinions, this book provides a fine analysis of the creation of Germany.

Taylor, A.J.P., *The Habsburg Monarchy 1809–1918* (Pelican, 1985; originally 1948). A customarily brilliant and predictably caustic examination of its subject.

Thomson, David, *Europe Since Napoleon* (Pelican, 1986). This work possesses all the virtues of the traditional history textbook, providing as it does a vast amount of information, combined with rigorous analysis.

Weiss, John, *Conservatism in Europe 1770–1945* (Thames and Hudson, 1977). An outstanding and brilliantly written introduction to the development of conservative thought, and its political expression.

Wilson, A.N. *The Victorians* (Hutchinson, 2002). The author is a successful journalist and novelist, two occupations which explain the high quality of his prose. This book provides a fine portrait of all aspects of the Victorian age, be they political, intellectual, or cultural.

MILITARY UNIFORMS

Haythornthwaite, Philip and Chappell, Michael *World Uniforms and Battles 1815–50* (Blandford, 1976). The Blandford Colour Series of illustrated military uniform books has acquired an almost legendary reputation. This particularly fine example is an essential source for the period in question.

Kannik, Preben, *Military Uniforms of the World in Colour* (Blandford, 1968). This book was one of the first to be published on its subject, and has proved itself to be of great use for wargamers ever since. It includes sixty-four colour illustrations of nineteenth-century European troops.

Kiley, Kevin F. and Smith, Digby, *An Illustrated Encyclopaedia of Military Uniforms of the Nineteenth Century* (Lorenz, 2010). This impressive volume contains colour illustrations of troops from the major European conflicts from the Crimean War to the Franco-Prussian War.

Marrion, Robert J., *Uniforms of the Franco-Prussian War, Volume 1: The Prussian Army 1870* (Partizan Press, 2008). This book is easily the best ever produced on its subject. It is to be hoped that further volumes in the series will follow.

North, René, *Military Uniforms, 1686–1918* (Hamlyn, 1970). Another renowned book of military uniforms, with particularly good coverage of nineteenth-century Europe.

Weaver, Ralph, *The Armies of the First Schleswig-Holstein War 1848–51* (Partizan Press, 2007). This is an essential book for anyone interested in its subject. It not only contains some fine colour illustrations, but also includes details of the relevant armies' organisation and equipment.

FIGURE PAINTING

Dallimore, Kevin, *Foundry Miniatures Painting and Modelling Guide* (Foundry, 2006). Anyone who aspires to paint wargames figures to a high standard should obtain a copy of this excellent book.

Appendix 2

Figure Sizes, Scales and Prices

Although the major figure sizes are 25mm, 20mm (for plastic figures), 15mm and 6mm, a vast range is now available. They are listed below, together with a description of their advantages and defects for wargaming purposes.

I have also provided a guide to how much an average army is likely to cost. This can obviously be seen as a very rough estimate, since prices inevitably change: they are only accurate at the time of writing. Nevertheless, the reader should have some idea how much he or she will have to pay for a generic wargames army, suitable for the standard scenarios given in Chapter 4. Armies for the minigame scenario will cost half the prices quoted.

(1) 54mm/1:32 scale. These figures were used by H.G. Wells in his book *Little Wars*, which started the wargaming hobby. For today's wargamers, metal figures in this scale are rather expensive (especially if the ready-painted toy soldiers are purchased). Plastic miniatures are much cheaper however, making wargaming in this scale a financially viable proposition.

The wargamer should be aware that whilst these figures look superb, they will need a very large table to deploy upon. A minimum of 240cm × 150cm (8′ × 5′) is advisable – or alternatively a back garden.

Current price per army: Painted metal figures, £1,500; Unpainted metal figures, £450; and Unpainted plastic figures, £60.

(2) 40/42mm. These provide a cheaper option of gaming with large scale metal figures than is possible with 54mm armies. However, as is the case with their larger brethren they do require a large wargames table.

Current price per army: £180.

(3) 25/28mm. This is the original metal wargaming size, and these figures look absolutely splendid when painted. Readers should however be aware that many manufacturers produce ranges of these miniatures, and that many vary in size. The more expensive figures in particular tend to be larger than their cheaper fellows (this increase in size allows designers to include fine detail in their miniatures). These large versions tend to be listed as 28mm rather than the more traditional 25mm – a broad convention that has been followed here. These larger figures may need to have bases larger than those suggested in the rules; in any event, all 25mm and 28mm armies fight best on larger tables: 180cm × 120cm. (6' × 4') is suggested.

Current price per army: 28mm, £150 and 25mm, £100. (Note: Readers should be warned that this price guide is even more approximate than the others listed: some 28mm figures will be cheaper, and 25mm products can conversely be rather more expensive.)

(4) 20mm/1:72 scale plastic figures. Although 1:72 scale actually measures at 25mm, it is a wargamers' convention to define plastic products (and a few metal miniatures of this size) as 20mm. This is in order to distinguish between 1:72 plastic and those metal figures listed as 25mm. Plastic figures have the advantage of being remarkably cheap and very lightweight (this is a big factor when transporting one's army to a friend's house or flat for a wargame). Battles can be fought on a table as small as 120cm × 90cm (4' × 3').

Current price per army: £30.

(5) 15mm. As outlined in *Wargaming: An Introduction*, these metal figures became necessary when huge wargames (of over 200 miniatures per army) were in fashion. They allow for fine detail to be painted on each figure, and do take up much less space than 25mm miniatures. They will never look quite as impressive as armies consisting of larger figures, but only need a table of 120cm × 90cm (4' × 3') for a viable game.

Current price per army: £35.

(6) 10mm. This new scale of metal miniatures has been popularised by Games Workshop's *Warmaster* fantasy game. I would suggest

using the same bases as for 15mm figures, but deploying double the number of 10mm miniatures on each. These miniatures are beginning to make their mark on the hobby, owing to the fact that they have enough detail to look impressive when painted, without having so much as to be difficult to paint. A 120cm × 90cm (4′ × 3′) table is appropriate.

Current price per army: £35.

(7) 6mm. These tiny figures were originally developed for World War Two wargames, in order to fit huge forces of tanks on small tables. Their use inevitably spread to other periods. Detailed painting is clearly impossible with such minute miniatures, but the main areas of the figures can be covered; and the armies do look very good en masse. I would suggest that the best option is to buy those figures that come ready based, as this saves time gluing miniatures to separate bases. 6mm battles can easily be fought on a table measuring 90cm × 60cm (3′ × 2′).

Current price per army: £12.

(8) 2mm. Unbelievable as it may seem, one company (Irregular Miniatures) really does produce figures and terrain of this size. Although mass battles can be fought using these miniatures, it is inevitably impossible to have any detailed painting on figures that are one step up from cardboard counters. I would suggest using four of the ready made 2mm bases to make up each unit, and halving all measurements listed in the rules. In this way, 2mm battles can be fought on tables measuring just 30cm × 30cm (1′ × 1′).

Current price per army: £4.

The reader will have observed that I have suggested different base and table sizes, depending on which scale of figure he or she prefers. This variation is so that the figures look right: squeezing 54mm armies on to a 120cm × 90cm (4′ × 3′) battlefield creates a somewhat farcical impression, for example. Similar aesthetic considerations apply to movement rules and firing ranges: battles with 25mm figures may benefit from using inches rather than centimetres; and 54mm miniatures could not only make a similar switch, but could also double all measurements (so that an Infantry unit would move 24 inches, rather than 12cm per turn).

Appendix 3

Useful Addresses

The following addresses, telephone numbers and website details (where applicable) will give the wargamer an idea of where to start collecting. Any enquiries by post should always be accompanied by a fairly large (A4 size) stamped addressed envelope (first class large letter stamp). This is because any catalogues (and sample figures) can weigh a fair amount, and therefore cost more than a standard letter to post. Do bear in mind that addresses and other contact details are liable to change. Also, note that many manufacturers are unable to receive personal callers, so do not on any account turn up on their doorstep!

MAGAZINES

These should be the first port of call for any wargamer. Both journals listed below should be available over the counter in most branches of W.H. Smith, and can in any case be ordered through any local newsagent. Subscription enquiries should be made to the following addresses:

Miniature Wargames, Subscriptions: West Street, Bourne, Lincolnshire, PE10 9PH
Tel: 01778 392494 – Web: www.miniwargames.com

Wargames Illustrated, Unit 26, Whitemoor Court Industrial Estate, Nottingham, NG8 5BY
Tel: 0115 929 5563 – Web: www.wargamesillustrated.net

These magazines are monthly publications. They contain excellent articles and are required reading for all wargamers. Moreover, all significant figure manufacturers advertise their latest releases in these journals, which provides another reason for buying them.

Battlegames, Battlegames Ltd, 17 Granville Road, Hove,
East Sussex, BN3 1TG
Tel: 01273 323320 – Web: www.battlegames.co.uk

This wargaming magazine is not (at the time of writing) available from W.H. Smith.
It is however a first class journal, which every wargamer should read. Copies can be
obtained from the address listed (above), as can subscriptions.

Wargames Recon, Stonehills, Unit 17, Shields Road, Pelaw,
Tyne and Wear, NE10 0HW
Tel: 0191 438 5585 – Web: www.wargamesrecon.co.uk

This new wargaming magazine is primarily devoted to in-depth reviews of wargames products. It cannot yet be purchased from W.H. Smith.

MILITARY BOOK SUPPLIERS

Caliver Books, 100 Baker Road, Newthorpe, Nottingham,
NG16 2DP
Tel: 0115 938 2111 – Web: www.caliverbooks.com

A vast range of new books and wargames rules can be obtained from this company.

David Lanchester's Military Books, 6 Pinfold Way,
Sherburn-in-elmet, North Yorkshire, LS25 6LF
Tel: 01977 684234 – Web: www.davidlanchestermilitarybooks.co.uk

This dealer is a splendid source for quality second hand books and new
publications at bargain prices.

Ken Trotman Ltd, PO Box 505, Huntingdon, PE29 2XW
Tel: 01480 454292 – Web: www.kentrotman.com

A fine range of new military history books can be obtained, but the firm are most
renowned for their vast second hand stock; and also their own publishing arm,
which produces a selection of primary source accounts.

Monarch Military Books and Miniatures, Unit 5a, Cuthbert Court,
Off Norwich Road, Dereham, Norfolk, NR19 1BX
Tel: 01362 691435 – Web: www.monarchmilitarybooks.com

This trader supplies wargames rules and new books – discounts are frequently
offered on the latter.

Paul Meekins Military and History Books, Valentines,
Long Marston, Stratford upon Avon, Warwickshire, CV37 8RG
Tel: 01789 722434 – Web: www.paulmeekins.co.uk

This dealer can be relied upon to supply many outstanding books that are no longer
in print, and is an especially good source for tracking down the wargaming classics.
He also sells all the major new releases.

MODEL FIGURE MANUFACTURERS

It should be noted that there are some excellent wargames figure companies arising all the time. It must not be assumed that I am listing all possible manufacturers in the list below. The companies in question are however some of the more prominent.

Baccus 6mm Ltd, Unit C, Graham House, Bardwell Road, Sheffield, S3 8AS
Tel: 0114 272 4491 – Web: www.baccus6mm.com
As the name suggests, Baccus only make 6mm figures, the quality of which is outstanding. They also produce an innovative set of wargames rules for the Franco-Prussian War.

Foundry Miniatures Ltd, 24–34 St Marks Street, Nottingham, NG3 1DE
Tel: 0115 841 3000 – Web: www.wargamesfoundry.com
Probably the largest figure company in the business, Foundry only make 28mm miniatures. They produce two large ranges, covering the Crimean and Franco-Prussian Wars.

Irregular Miniatures, 41 Lesley Avenue, York, YO10 4JR
Tel: 01904 671101 – Web: www.irregularminiatures.co.uk
Irregular are in many ways a unique company, in that they produce a huge selection in every single available size of figure. All ranges are moreover remarkably cheap, and their mail order service is probably the most efficient in the hobby.

Miniature Figurines (see address for Caliver Books).
This famous name from the history of wargaming now has its figures produced by Caliver Books. Two 15mm ranges are available for this period, covering the Crimean and Franco-Prussian Wars.

North Star Military Figures Ltd, Unit W37, Lenton Business Centre, Lenton Boulevard, Nottingham NG7 2BY
Tel: 0115 978 6656 – Web: www.northstarfigures.com
This company owns and sells The Great War Miniatures and Helion figure ranges (both 28mm), covering the Crimean War and Seven Weeks War respectively.

Pendraken Miniatures, 1 Easby Grove, Eston, Middlesbrough, T56 9DL
Tel: 01642 460638 – Web: www.pendraken.co.uk
This 10mm specialist has a huge selection of figures, covering all the major European conflicts from the Crimean War through to the Russo-Turkish War.

QRF Models Ltd, Unit 2, Gibbs Marsh Farm, Stalbridge, Dorset, DT10 2RU
Tel: 01963 363521 – Web: www.quickreactionforce.co.uk
This company produces the huge Freikorps range of 15mm figures. All the major European conflicts from 1848 through 1871 are covered.

Spencer Smith Miniatures, The Old Rectory, Wortham, Diss, Norfolk, IP22 1SL
Tel: 01379 650021 – Web: www.spencersmithminiatures.co.uk
This company has started to produce a range of 30mm figures covering the Franco-Prussian War. They also supply the famous Willie and Tradition 30mm figures, along with 25mm miniatures from the latter company. In addition, an incredibly wide selection of 42mm figures from a company named Shiny Toy Soldiers is marketed by Spencer Smith.

PLASTIC FIGURE STOCKISTS
Harfields Military Figure Specialists, 32 St Winifreds Road, Biggin Hill, Westerham, Kent, TN16 3HP
Tel: 01959 576269 – Web: www.harfields.com
Although the local toy or (if the reader is lucky enough to have access to one) model shop will always supply plastic figures, Harfields are guaranteed to fill in any gaps. A range of sale items, and out of production second hand figures (some of which are in mint condition) are also available.

WARGAMES TERRAIN MAUNFACTURERS
Magister Militum, Unit 4, The Business Centre, Morgans Vale Road, Redlynch, Salisbury, SP5 2HA
Tel: 01725 510 110 – Web: www.magistermilitum.com
A vast selection of scenery is available both pre-painted and unpainted.

MILITARY HISTORY SOCIETIES
The Continental Wars Society, Ralph Weaver, 37 Yeading Avenue, Rayners Lane, Harrow, Middlesex, HA2 9RL.
Tel: 020 8868 1081
This society is devoted solely to nineteenth-century European warfare from 1815 onwards. It covers both military history and wargaming, in a truly outstanding bimonthly newsletter. Anyone with an interest in this fascinating period should join.

Index

Alexander, Prince of Hesse 83, 147, 148
Arentschildt, General von 147
Armies:
  Austrian 9, 67–8, 74, 78–9, 117–18,
    124–5, 126–7, 140, 142–4
  Bavarian 81–2, 147, 151–2
  British 66–7, 71–2, 97–9, 106, 109
  Danish 69–70, 76–7, 124, 127–8, 131,
    134
  Federal German 82–3, 147
  French 16, 73–4, 84–6, 106, 117–18, 157,
    158, 161–2, 171–2
  Garibaldini 74–5
  Hanoverian 81, 147, 148
  Italian 9, 68–9, 83–4
  Monarchical 64–5
  Neapolitan 75–6
  Ottoman Turk 87–8
  Prussian 16, 70–1, 77–8, 79–81, 86, 130,
    131, 132–3, 139–40
  Revolutionary 63–4
  Russian 72–3, 87, 106, 110
  Schleswig-Holstein 70–1
  Spanish Carlist 65–6, 95–6, 100–1
  Spanish Cristino 66–7, 94–5, 101–2
Alvensleben, General Konstantin von
  159–60

Battles:
  Alegria 92–6
  Alma, the 104–12
  Custoza 83–4, 139
  Kissingen 147–54
  Königgrätz 142
  Magenta 115–16
  Mars-La-Tour 19, 155–65
  Montebello 113–21

  Nachod 137–46
  Oeversee 122–9
  Oriamendi 97–103
  Rackebull 130–6
  Sedan 166–73
  Solferino 115–16
Bazaine, Marshal Achille 157–61, 167,
  168, 169, 172
Benedek, General Ludwig von 79, 139,
  140, 142
Benedetti, Count Vincente 156
Bismarck, Otto von 12, 20, 123, 138, 150,
  156–7, 160, 169
Borbon, General Don Sebastian de 99
Bredow, General Friedrich Wilhelm
  von 19, 86, 161, 169

Carl, Prince of Bavaria 147, 148, 152
Cavour, Count Camillo di 113, 116–17
Clausewitz, Carl von 12–14
Communism 10–11
Conservatism 3–4, 8, 12, 20, 65

Dunant, Henri 116

Engels, Fredrich 10–11
Evans, General George de Lacy 98–100

Falckenstein, General Eduard Vogel
  von 139, 147, 148, 149
Featherstone, Donald 37, 91
Forey, General 115
Friedrich Carl, Prince of Prussia 130

Gablenz, General Leopold von 79, 125,
  141
Garibaldi, Guiseppe 74–5, 86, 116–17

Gerlach, General 130–1
Goeben, General von 131, 148–9
Griffith, Paddy 90

Jeffrey, George 29
Jomini, Antoine Henri 5–6, 7–8, 12–13

Kriegspiel 16, 30, 90

Liberalism 3–4, 8–9, 11, 64, 67, 69, 75, 138

MacMahon, Marshal Patrice 158, 159,
    161, 166–8, 172
Marx, Karl 10–11
Menshikov, Prince 105–6
Metternich, Klemens von 3–4, 5, 8–9
Meza, General Christian Julius de 124,
    130
Moltke, General Helmuth von 15, 77,
    79–81, 139–40, 147, 148, 149, 166,
    167–8
Müller, Colonel Max 125–6, 127–8

Napoleon I, Emperor of France xii, 3,
    14, 39, 155
Napoleon III, Emperor of France 85,
    113, 116, 123, 155–7, 167, 169
Nationalism 3–4, 9, 11–12, 13–14, 64, 69,
    138
Nightingale, Florence 108

O'Doyle, General 93

Palmerston, Viscount 97, 122
Picq, Ardant du 12, 15, 19, 21, 159

Radetzky, Field Marshal 67–8, 69, 74,
    113, 114

Raglan, Lord 106–7
Ramming, General Wilhelm von 140–1
Reisswitz, Lieutenant B. von 16
Russell, William Howard 108

Schleswig-Holstein Question 122–3,
    132, 137, 139
Stadion, General 115
Steinmetz, General Karl von 140, 141,
    166

Vienna, Congress of 3–4, 8, 11, 12, 14,
    170

Wargaming:
  Army Lists 61–88
  Design Principles 23–41
  Rules 42–9, 62–3
  Scenarios 50–60
Wars:
  American Civil 21, 87
  Carlist 65–7, 92–3, 100
  Crimean 71–3, 104–5, 108–9
  First Schleswig 69–71, 122
  Franco-Austrian 73–4, 113–14, 116
  Franco-Prussian 16, 21, 84–6, 155–9,
      166–8, 169–70
  Italian Independence 67–9, 74–6,
      113–14, 115–17
  Russo-Turkish 20, 87–8
  Second Schleswig 76–9, 122–4, 131–2
  Seven Weeks 78–84, 137–9, 149–50
Wellington, Duke of 97
Wesencraft, C.F. 90
Wilhelm I, King of Prussia 156, 169

Zumalacárregui, General 93